FINDING THE WEST

Histories of the American Frontier

JAMES P. RONDA

Finding the West

EXPLORATIONS WITH LEWIS AND CLARK

University of New Mexico Press   Albuquerque

Library of Congress Cataloging-in-Publication Data

Ronda, James P., 1943–

Finding the West : explorations with Lewis and Clark / James P.

Ronda.—1st ed.

p.   cm.—(Histories of the American frontier)

Includes bibliographical references and index.

ISBN 0-8263-2417-7 (alk. paper)

1. Lewis and Clark Expedition (1804–1806)

2. Lewis, Meriwether, 1774–1809—Literary art.

3. Clark, William, 1770–1838—Literary art.

4. West (U.S.)—Folklore.

5. West (U.S.)—Discovery and exploration.

6. West (U.S.)—Description and travel.

7. Storytelling—West (U.S.)—History—19th century.

8. Frontier and pioneer life in literature.

I. Title. II. Series.

F592.7 .R65 2001

917.804'2—dc21   2001001226

For Jeanne
With thanks for all the journeys and all the stories

Contents

Foreword
Course of Discovery

In the annals of American exploration, no single journey looms larger in either history or myth than the celebrated expedition that between 1804 and 1806 carried Meriwether Lewis, William Clark, and more than three dozen companions from the Mississippi River to the mouth of the Columbia and back again. Commissioned by no less a patron than Thomas Jefferson to compile detailed maps, descriptions, and scientific data regarding the newly acquired Louisiana Purchase, the famed "Corps of Discovery" in fact did much more. In addition to the substantive information that it added to American knowledge of the West—information about geography, geology, native peoples, flora and fauna, merchantable commodities, and possible routes to the Pacific Ocean—the Lewis and Clark Expedition became a defining symbol of the national frontier, so much so that its very name has become synonymous with exploration. The historical narrative began with the journals of the explorers themselves, received its initial canonical form in the edition put together in 1814 by Nicholas Biddle, and has been retold endlessly—in histories, popular fictions, movies, and scholarly monographs—ever since. It remains among the most essential stories of the American past.

Of the many scholars who have contributed to our understanding of the expedition, from Reuben Gold Thwaites to Bernard DeVoto to Gary Moulton to Stephen Ambrose, James Ronda has been an especially creative and insightful interpreter. His *Lewis and Clark Among the Indians* is the classic work on this subject, enabling us to see as never before the complex, subtle interactions between Lewis and Clark and the native peoples through whose homelands the expedition journeyed. His *Astoria and Empire* enables us to see the larger economic and imperial framework that shaped the goals and assumptions within which journeys of exploration like this one took place. And his many essays and edited volumes have probed into the minds and lives of the expedition as few have done before him.

Finding the West is something of a departure for Jim Ronda, a more intimate, playful, and personal engagement with the subject to which he has devoted so much of his scholarly career. Those of us who are lucky enough to know Jim personally understand that his talents go far beyond the painstaking archival research and scrupulous interpretive analysis that are the hallmarks of everything he does. He is, for instance, a deeply committed, indeed, passionate undergraduate teacher whose lectures surely count among the most cherished memories for any student fortunate enough to stumble into his classroom. Jim never walks to the podium without bringing with him an extraordinary energy and enthusiasm for whatever subject he is discussing, so that one comes to the end of his lectures surprised that the time has gone so quickly, and regretful that it has ended so soon. *Finding the West* has the great virtue of capturing more of Jim's skill as a teacher than any other book he has produced, so that those who read it can look forward to watching a great teacher at work.

But Jim is more than a teacher. He is a master storyteller as well, a storyteller who never forgets that big ideas and abstract arguments are always incarnated in the flesh and blood of living human beings, whether those human beings are explorers far out on the western frontier, or subsequent scholars and editors interpreting what those explorers might have been thinking and doing out there. Jim's generous empathy with the many different people whose stories he tells has always been one of the special hallmarks of his scholarship. But in this book he goes further. Beyond the Lewis and Clark Expedition, his deeper subject is storytelling itself: the many ways in which the tales we tell about the Corps of Discovery constantly reshape the meanings we extract from it, and how they help define the different moral compasses we use in seeking to understand our own lives as well.

In contrast to the gripping but rather traditional heroic narrative that Stephen Ambrose constructed about Lewis and Clark in his book *Undaunted Courage*, Jim Ronda offers a series of meditations in which different aspects of the expedition become the occasion for reflecting on the many ways it continues to resonate in our national consciousness. What he offers is at once less familiar and more intriguing than the familiar account we have all heard many times before. In Ronda's confident hands, the expedition becomes a kaleidoscope through which we can contemplate not just the significance of this key moment in western history, but the multitudinous ways we can understand it, and the ways our changing understandings can serve in turn as exemplars for history itself. It is a masterful performance by one of the leading historians of the American West today, the work of a great teacher who is also a gifted writer and a consummate storyteller.

William Cronon,
University of Wisconsin,
for the editors of the
Histories of the American Frontier series

Coeditors:
Howard R. Lamar, Yale University
Martin Ridge, The Huntington Library
David J. Weber, Southern Methodist University

Preface

"Many Extroadenary Stories"

On a bright, windy day in mid-October 1804, William Clark joined inter-preter Joseph Gravelines and a prominent Arikara chief for a quiet walk along the Missouri River shore. It was part ramble, part reconnaissance—just the sort of thing Clark had done before and would do again in the days to come. The night before, with the Corps of Discovery camped along the river in what is now Sioux county, North Dakota, Arikaras from the vil-lages lower down the river had come to visit the Americans. Perhaps notic-ing that expedition cooking pots were not completely full, two Indians had returned with pronghorn and buffalo meat. Soon the autumn air was filled with the smell and sizzle of good food shared around the fire. Clark re-membered the evening fondly, writing that "those Indians Stayed all night, they Sung and was verry merry the greater part of the night."[1] Memories of a troubled confrontation with the Teton Sioux just weeks before now faded in the smoky pleasures of a river camp. The following morning, as a stiff northwest wind halted progress up river, Clark and his companions were ready to take a look at the country ahead.

What Clark and his friends first saw on their hike was a river world teem-ing with animal life. Everywhere they looked there were "large gangues" of buffalo, elk, and pronghorn. Gravelines, who knew the country well, told Clark stories about those animals, their migrations, and where they lived during the severe Great Plains winters. Gravelines' stories were explana-tions about a landscape Clark believed he understood and appreciated already. The Arikara chief, known to Lewis and Clark and Thomas Jefferson as Arketarnarshar, or "chief of the town," also told stories along the way.[2] Like Gravelines, he had explored the country and made his own narrative map. But these were narratives that first composed and then explained a very different landscape. "This chief," Clark later recalled, "tells me of a number of their Treditions about Turtles, Snakes etc, and the power of a perticiler rock or Cave on the next river which informs of everr thing." Clark listened patiently to those "extroadenary stories" but then dismissed them as not "worth while mentioning."[3]

Although he may not have recognized it, everything Clark heard that morning was about landscapes, their exploration, creation, and many meanings. As the dean of landscape scholars John Brinckerhoff Jackson explains, a landscape is "a man-made system of spaces superimposed on the face of the land."[4] That "system of spaces" is created not only by building on the land or changing the terrain but by telling stories about the meanings of those constructions. As Barry Lopez tells us, narrative calls landscape into being. Words gather up terrain, shape it, and make it a landscape. Hearing Nunamiut hunters from Alaska's Brooks Range tell about their experiences with wolverines, Lopez found that "the landscape seemed alive because of the stories."[5] Joseph Gravelines fashioned a landscape of animals, changing seasons, and the movements of hunter and prey. This was a vision of the world that fit Lewis and Clark's assumptions and expectations. Animals moved in a landscape defined by human desire, and the future could only be dimly seen in the yearly currents of weather and the seasons. In the months to come, expedition journals were filled with such landscape stories—stories that became part of the invention of the American West.

The Arikara stories Clark named and then shrugged off were about animals and the land but with a compelling difference. Arketarnarshar sketched out a world in which the boundary between the visible and the invisible, the natural and the supernatural, first blurred and then vanished. A story about a turtle might tell of one particular animal or it could suggest the relationship between what turtles represent and humankind. One Arikara story still current in modern times has a giant turtle teaching a group of young hunters about respect for things that are sacred and powerful.[6] These stories not only conjured up animal landscapes; they took certain terrain features and invested them with larger meanings. The Arikara future-telling rock—probably a reference to Medicine Hill in Grant County, North Dakota—was widely recognized by Missouri River peoples as a unique point in the landscape. Several Mandans told Clark about the rock, assuring him that those who ventured there in the spring or summer and performed the proper rituals would be rewarded with revelations about "every thing which is to happen."[7] Like the turtle and snake stories, the rock narratives were ways of creating landscapes. The stories were not only acts of creation; they were verbal maps that located native people in time and place.

Arketarnarshar and Gravelines were storytellers, and in their own way they were explorers as well. What they shared with Clark entered the American exploration record, enriching it and us. Their words created landscapes and ways of seeing and interpreting them. These narrators lived lives in those narratives and invited listeners to join them in worlds fashioned by "extroadenary stories." But "storyteller" is not a word we easily apply to explorers, whether Euro-American or Native American. We think it makes more sense to describe them as naturalists, cartographers, ethnographers, documentary artists, or diplomats in the service of empire. Perhaps our reluctance to call explorers storytellers has something to do with the reputation of the word "story." The slang expression "what's your story?" tells it all. Story has become another word for alibi, something between truth and falsehood. We do not expect storytellers to consider and report accurately on "true" things. Stories are for bedtime; they are moments of fantasy, escape, and happy endings. We sometimes dismiss Homer's *Odyssey* or the exodus of Moses and the Jews from Egypt as "just stories" belonging to a realm of meaning remote from real life. But in recent times writers like Barry Lopez, Sherman Alexie, Mary Clearman Blew, and Bill Kittredge have rediscovered the power of stories as narrative and explanation. As Kittredge says in a compelling essay on narrative and the West, stories are "maps or paradigms in which we see our purposes defined."[8]

Explorers made their journeys of whatever distance, saw what they could, and came home to tell about it. Some offered astounding fabrications—reports of inland seas, golden cities, and blond Indians. Others told about shining mountains, boiling mud pots, and vast herds of shaggy animals in a sea of grass. Made at that place where imagination meets experience, those were the stories that came back at journey's end. But those same stories were intimately connected to the ones told before leaving home. Modern readers will quickly recognize that many of those stories were the very ones that prompted voyages of discovery. Explorers saw what seemed to them new lands and strange peoples through the "home-told stories." As historical geographer D. W. Meinig reminds us, "landscape is composed not only of what lies before our eyes but lies within our heads."[9] And what explorers from the new American republic had in their heads ranged from grand narratives of revolution and independence to tales about the nature

of Nature and the character of human beings in a world that seemed at
once very old and marvelously new. Native American explorers, struggling
to understand a landscape transformed by epidemic disease, European trade
goods and firearms, and the imperial ambitions of newly-arrived strangers,
had their own vocabulary of images and traditions. Indians explored the
explorers, making what we sometimes blandly call "exploration" an act
of mutual discovery. Like their Euro-American counterparts, Native
American explorers used exploration stories rooted in age-old experience
to explain a world suddenly new and often unpredictable. The explorer as
storyteller lived between two narratives—the "home-told" story and "what
I saw out there" story. Desire and imagination, passion and speculation
fueled them both, and joined to create western landscapes.

   This is a book about many storytellers. The voices heard here come in
many languages and accents. The words are French-Canadian, Shoshone,
New Hampshire English, Hidatsa, and Chinookan. In their journals and
on their maps, Lewis and Clark tried to capture those many voices and
their varied inflections. Doing that, they told stories about themselves, the
people they met on their "road across the continent," and what President
Jefferson called "the face of the country." They repeated stories gathered
from others and sometimes created new ones. Lewis and Clark lived inside large and important stories about passages, gardens, empires, and re-
publics. At the same time they could not escape the cultural inheritance
of age-old legends about heroes, quests, and noble sacrifice. But it would
be a mistake to think that Lewis and Clark moved only in storied realms
of glory, marching roads trod by ancient heroes and venerable pilgrims.
The life of any exploring party held more routine than excitement, more
that was commonplace than promised high adventure. Day-by-day there
were smaller but no less important ones about food, weather, and personal
memory. Sergeant John Ordway shaped part of what we know about the
Arikara landscape when he recalled helpings of beans and corn, saying "we
Eat Some of each and found it verry Good."[10] William Clark recounted a
memorable piece of the Columbia River story when he described the river
tumbling through the Short and Long Narrows of The Dalles with "the
horrid appearance of this agitated gut Swelling, boiling and whirling in
every direction."[11] Meriwether Lewis put himself in the landscape story
when, struggling up the Missouri near Three Forks, his men praised him
for learning "to push a tolerable good pole."[12] And the expedition's French
boatmen put their own imprint on the western landscape when they reported that the loud boomings heard around the Great Falls of the

Missouri were actually "the bursting of the rich mines of silver which these mountains contain."[13]

The rich and varied stories that the Lewis and Clark journals hold are at the heart of this book. Some of those accounts—most often the ones featuring Lewis and Clark in heroic pose—have passed into the national consciousness, shaping visions of the West expressed in painting, literature, public policy, and personal memory. But the most resonant are not the simple tales, recounting the adventures of a few white men sent into the West by one ambitious American president. For every story told by travelers there are a dozen from those who stayed at home or watched as the adventurers passed by. Thomas Jefferson told stories about the western country that were filled with hopeful geography, marvelous animals, and a promising American future. Artisans and outfitters in Philadelphia like seamstress Matilda Chapman and tobacconist Thomas Leiper, Jr. had their own expedition stories, even if the exact words and plots are now lost to us. In St. Louis, Antoine Pierre Soulard's map told a western story, as did the words and experiences of river explorer James Mackay and the shadowy Captain John McClellan.

Native American exploration narratives abound in the Lewis and Clark record, sometimes hinted at and other times told in great detail. Arketarnarshar was not the only Arikara storyteller to fashion a geography made of words and imagination. Soon after the Corps of Discovery left the Arikara villages, trader Pierre-Antoine Tabeau heard a fascinating set of stories about the Americans and their mission. Village people imagined that Lewis and Clark were on a special vision quest. That hazardous journey brought the travelers face to face with "obstacles perhaps invincible," including a terrible, smoke-breathing beast and "a troop of Amazons who kill all their male children, pulverize their genitals and conceive again by the injection of the powder obtained."[14] While Tabeau may have mixed some of his own cultural baggage and tale-telling with the Arikara stories, when he poked fun at the native accounts he was sharply reproved by the Indians. During the Fort Mandan winter there was ample time for earth lodge people and fort people to investigate each other and fashion narrative landscapes. The Mandan chief Black Cat was a regular visitor at the American post and often told Clark "many Indian anickdotes."[15] Black Cat not only told stories, he asked the kinds of questions all explorers ask. As Clark recalled, Black Cat "made Great inquiries respecting our fashions."[16] Shoshone headman Cameahwait brought the northern plains landscape to life when he described a world filled with firearms in the hands of hostile neighbors. "If we had guns," Cameahwait graphically put it, "we could then live in the country of the buffaloe and eat as our enemies do and not be compelled to hide ourselves in these mountains and live on roots and berries as the bear do."[17]

The stories in *Finding the West* are bound together by the power of imagination and desire, encounter and experience. Euro-American explorers in the Age of Thomas Jefferson and Sir Joseph Banks might have thought themselves Reason's children, but passion was everywhere in their lives. As Captain George Vancouver admitted, he and his fellow adventurers were caught up in the "ardour of the present age, to discover and delineate the true geography of the earth."[18] Imagination fashioned maps that were guides to countries of enchantment and renewal. Desire for wealth, security, fame, knowledge, and power drove explorers to find what imagination created. Jefferson's captains went up the Missouri and into the West in search of ideas shaped by imagination and born of desire. The idea of the passage, the idea of the garden, the idea of a republican West, the idea of a western wonderland—all these seemed waiting to be found in shapes of earth, rock and water just over the horizon. Looking for ideas in an imagined landscape, Lewis and Clark encountered a western geography with all the complexities and ambiguities that we meet when we try to navigate "real" places like airports, freeways, shopping malls, and parking decks.

The Lewis and Clark expedition was not simply imagination's army marching through fantasy's landscape without consequences for itself, the western country, and those who already called the West home. Images of change and transformation filled the stories Lewis and Clark told about themselves and their journey. Lewis and Clark saw themselves as representatives of a changing world. They embraced change, celebrated it, and made it visible in military parades, treaty talks, and trade goods. New economies, new objects, and a new Great Father gave shape and substance to exploration stories. Even when Lewis and Clark told native people that nothing was going to change in their lives, it was plain that many important things were changing. The questions native people asked were about change as well. Whoever the storyteller, whether native or newcomer, the story was now about the winds of change. The stories in *Finding the West* are meant to remind us about the course of events after Lewis and Clark "found" what they thought was their West. The stories they told—and the ones we tell about them—had enduring consequences. Describing Coboway's people as "low," "badly made," and "illy formed," somehow made it easier in later years to evict Clatsops from their lands on the Columbia.[19] Garden stories shaped federal homestead legislation, colored railroad promotional advertising, and lured my Dutch immigrant family in the 1890s to seek Jefferson's rural paradise in southern Colorado. Tales of the expedition as national triumph lent legitimacy to what the distinguished historian Francis Jennings once called "the cant of conquest."

And in our own time there are some who insist on recounting the journey as manly adventure wrapped in heroic courage, denying the travelers their humanity as fallible, often complaining human beings. There was courage along the way but there was also complaint. No one was more honest about that than William Clark. Struggling to find a navigable channel in the shoal-choked Beaverhead River, Clark's men "complain[ed] verry much of the emence labour they are obliged to undergo and wish much to leave the river."[20] Clark made no effort to hide those feelings from the pages of his journal; Nicholas Biddle, the expedition's first editor, told a much less powerful story, saying merely that the explorers were "very anxious to commence traveling by land."[21] In recent years some have been tempted to reconstruct the Lewis and Clark journey as a national epic with places, words, and roles for all Americans. Nations need shared stories but telling the Lewis and Clark journey as a single narrative promising common ground for all ignores the profound historical, cultural and ethnic differences in this and all other exploration experiences. Denying such differences only widens the cultural divide, producing a national history that speaks in one master voice and allows only one predetermined conclusion. What we say about the many meanings of the Lewis and Clark stories matters as much as what we say about slavery, the Civil War, and the social movements of the 1960s.

Finding the West offers stories of moral consequence. They ask us to think again about one notable journey in our past and then consider the larger, longer meanings in that voyage. Such a reconsideration might reveal not one voyage but many, not one band of explorers but whole congregations of the intrepid and the curious. The history of North America has been shaped—some would say even defined—by travelers and their stories. Our earliest literature, both Native American and Euro-American, is filled with tales of journey-making and exploration. To revisit Lewis and Clark is to look again at all those who left home to find something of value some other place. Going in search of Lewis and Clark and the West they sought to find, we are sure to encounter Cherokees and Creeks on the way to Indian Territory, Norwegian farmers bound for Minnesota, and African Americans leaving Clarksdale, Mississippi for the promised land in Chicago. Explorers question the earth, seeking answers about the meanings of the present and the contours of the future. Lewis and Clark did that; so did Arketarnarshar, Black Cat, Cameahwait, Sacagawea, and Coboway.

Don Jackson once described his *Thomas Jefferson and the Stony Mountains: Exploring the West from Monticello* as "an aspect book." By that he meant that it was neither a Jefferson biography nor a full-scale history of western exploration in the first two decades of the nineteenth century. What Don offered was a book about one part of Jefferson's spacious mind and its relationship to the American West. *Finding the West* is my "aspect book." It is not a retelling of the familiar Lewis and Clark story. Instead, it invites readers to make several kinds of Lewis and Clark journeys. Some are physical and directional, traversing the American landscape from Monticello to the Clatsop village at the mouth of the Columbia River. Others suggest ventures of the mind and imagination, recognizing that Lewis and Clark explored countries of dream and expectation. These chapters are, as the book's subtitle says, *"explorations with Lewis and Clark,"* not retracings of familiar routes. They take the trails less traveled. Some began as public lectures, and my thanks go to friends and friendly audiences at Montana State University, the University of Washington, Fort Clatsop National Memorial, and the Gilcrease Museum. Other chapters were written specifically for this book. Only three have previously appeared in print, though each was slightly revised for this book, and I gratefully acknowledge permission to reprint: James P. Ronda, "A Moment in Time: The West—September 1806," *Montana, The Magazine of Western History* (vol. 44, autumn 1994): 2–15; Ronda, "A Promise of Rivers: Thomas Jefferson and the Exploration of Western Waterways," in *Frontier and Region: Essays in Honor of Martin Ridge*, edited by Robert C. Ritchie and Paul Andrew Hutton (Albuquerque: University of New Mexico Press, 1997); Ronda, "Coboway's Tale," in *Power and Place in the North American West*, edited by Richard White and John M. Findlay (Seattle: University of Washington Press, 1999).

In *The Good Old Boys*, Elmer Kelton's masterful novel set in 1905, young Cotton Calloway envisions a twentieth-century Texas filled with automobiles, airplanes, and other mechanical marvels. For Cotton, the future is a landscape filled with factories and machines. He is eager to be part of building it. Cotton's uncle Hewey has seen part of the future in places like Fort Worth and doubts its promise. "I hope you like it when you get it finished," he tells Cotton in what is plainly the novel's most memorable line.[22] As we consider the western landscapes created by the whole range of exploration stories, we might join Cotton and Hewey to ask our own questions about the character and destiny of the western country.

Notes

1. Gary E. Moulton, ed., *The Journals of the Lewis and Clark Expedition,* 12 vols. (Lincoln: University of Nebraska Press, 1983–2000), 3: 177. Hereafter cited as JLCE.

2. There remains some confusion about this Arikara's proper name. Arketarnarshar or "chief of the town" may have been his title. Gary Moulton suggests that his name was Eagles Feather. This Arikara chief traveled with Lewis and Clark to meet with the Mandans in 1804; he was later part of a delegation that went to Washington, D.C. in 1805. His untimely death there was one more cause for mounting tension between Arikaras and Americans.

3. JLCE, 3: 179–80.

4. John Brinckerhoff Jackson, *Discovering the Vernacular Landscape* (New Haven: Yale University Press, 1984), 8.

5. Barry Lopez, *Crossing Open Ground* (New York: Random House, 1978), 63.

6. Douglas R. Parks, ed., *Traditional Narratives of the Arikara Indians,* 4 vols. (Lincoln: University of Nebraska Press, 1991), 3: 287–89.

7. JLCE, 3: 299.

8. William Kittredge, "The Politics of Storytelling," in Deborah Clow and Donald Snow, eds., *Northern Lights* (New York: Random House, 1994), 42.

9. D. W. Meinig, "The Beholding Eye: Ten Versions of the Same Scene," in D. W. Meinig, ed., *The Interpretation of Ordinary Landscapes* (New York: Oxford University Press, 1979), 34.

10. JLCE, 9: 79.

11. Ibid., 5: 333.

12. Ibid., 4: 423.

13. Ibid., 4: 375.

14. Annie Heloise Abel, ed., *Tabeau's Narrative of Loisel's Expedition to the Upper Missouri* (Norman: University of Oklahoma Press, 1939), 200–201.

15. JLCE, 3: 240.

16. Ibid., 3: 237. Mandan and Hidatsa exploration strategies are discussed at length in James P. Ronda, "Exploring the Explorers: Great Plains Peoples and the Lewis and Clark Expedition," in Ronda, ed., *Voyages of Discovery: Essays on the Lewis and Clark Expedition* (Helena: Montana Historical Society Press, 1998), 183–99.

17. JLCE, 5: 91.
18. George Vancouver, *A Voyage of Discovery to the North Pacific Ocean and Round the World, 1791–95*, 4 vols., W. Kaye Lamb, ed. (London, 1798; reprint, Cambridge, England: The Hakluyt Society, 1984), 1: 275.
19. James P. Ronda, *Lewis and Clark among the Indians* (Lincoln: University of Nebraska Press, 1984), 203.
20. JLCE, 5: 76.
21. Nicholas Biddle, *History of the Expedition under the Command of Captains Lewis and Clark*, 2 vols. (Philadelphia, 1814; reprint in 3 vols. with additional notes by Elliott Coues, New York: Francis P. Harper, 1898), 2: 486.
22. Elmer Kelton, *The Good Old Boys* (1978; reprint, Fort Worth: Texas Christian University Press, 1985), 64.

Acknowledgments

No words about the Lewis and Clark Expedition have been more important to me over the past twenty years than these from my mentor and friend Donald Jackson. "It is no longer useful to think of the Lewis and Clark Expedition as the personal story of two men. Their journey to the Pacific and return in 1804–6 was an enterprise of many aims and a product of many minds." Don's words continue to expand and deepen the Lewis and Clark story, making it many stories, and giving voice to travelers and adventurers as different as a young soldier from New Hampshire, a Philadelphia seamstress, a Clatsop chief, and an attorney general of the United States. Don Jackson showed me a Corps of Discovery larger than Thomas Jefferson ever imagined. It was John Allen who first opened my eyes to appreciate exploration landscapes both real and imagined. No one has taught me more about "seeing" the West as the country of the mind. While I was not trained as an historical geographer, John has made me feel welcome in that adventuresome company.

In all of this—whether on the trail or in the library—I have been heartened and supported by good friends and congenial places to work. Gary Moulton, Carolyn Gilman, Bill Cronon, Chuck Rankin, Martha Kohl, Al Furtwangler, and Bill Lang have always been ready when I needed a word of encouragement, advice, or just the next word. By way of their books, Bernard DeVoto, Barry Lopez, Elmer Kelton, and Bill Kittredge remain a constant presence in my life. I am grateful for their words and examples. Historians live in a country of words. While I cherish my citizenship in that republic, I have also been a traveler in the world of jazz. I gratefully acknowledge my debt to Duke Ellington, Louis Armstrong, Jelly Roll Morton, Bix Beiderbecke, and Benny Goodman for inspiration and solace in boundless measure. Over the past decade I have found the Special Collections Department at the University of Tulsa's McFarlin Library to be both workplace and homeplace. Lori N. Curtis and her staff have met my every need—whether for fresh coffee or an obscure document—with genuine friendship and real enthusiasm for my work. And in England there is no place dearer to my heart than Wroxton College in Oxfordshire. Each summer, college dean Dr. Nicholas Baldwin, F.R.S., has made a place for my wife Jeanne and me to read, write, and share stories. Our lives have been immeasurably enhanced by his good cheer and Wroxton's quiet ways. I owe a special debt of thanks to Head Groundskeeper Robert Denton who taught me that watching badgers or hunting for old railway lines is yet another way to read the landscape and learn its lessons.

Every book is a collaboration between author and editor. *Finding the West* was called into being by the skill, imagination, and good graces of David Holtby at the University of New Mexico Press. David suggested this book, encouraged its writing, and brought it to press. He was patient where patience was needed; he was encouraging where encouragement mattered; he was insistent where prodding was required. For all of that I am genuinely grateful.

This book is a voyage of exploration into a large and complex American story. Willa Cather said that there are only two or three human stories, and we repeat them endlessly. The Lewis and Clark journey is one of those stories. Repeating the story can deepen it and enrich us. That has always been my hope. For more than thirty years Jeanne and I have been sharing our own journey stories. This book is for her as a celebration of our years together and her presence in my life.

For what is good here I take only modest credit; for what slips off the trail I take full responsibility.

Tulsa, Oklahoma
November 2000

ONE

A Promise of Rivers

Thomas Jefferson and the Exploration of Western Waterways

Sometime during the year 1800 Thomas Jefferson paused to take stock of his services to the young American republic. The memorandum list he drafted held the predictable: the Declaration of Independence, legislation concerning personal liberty, and experiments with useful plants and domestic animals. But at the head of the list Jefferson put something modern readers are sure to find disconcerting. Pride of place went to Jefferson's prolonged efforts at making the Rivanna River a navigable waterway.[1] While mountain tops and elevated views attracted the Virginian, rivers fascinated him. Their promise—both as routes for expansion and ties to bind West to East—became the central metaphor for all Jefferson's western plans. To follow Jefferson's rivers is to trace the courses and currents of a republic bound for empire, and often bound up in the troubles of empire.

Rivers had long figured in the dreams and schemes of European explorers and their ambitious patrons. Schooled in images drawn from the early chapters of Genesis, Europeans understood rivers as both passages to wealth and as symbols of its presence. As the biblical writer proclaimed, "a river went out of Eden to water the garden."[2] Columbus and his contemporaries looked at American rivers and saw more than passageways. Rivers were signs, messages from the interior about the nature and meaning of the New World. Searching for the paradise of Eden on his third voyage in 1498, Columbus found great rivers flowing out to the sea. Marveling at the delta of the Orinoco—"so great and deep a river"—the navigator was sure it signaled paradise close at hand.[3] Other adventurers who came later were less convinced about the nearness of Eden. Because they imagined the continent a barrier on the way to the fabled Orient, rivers became the centerpiece in the endless search for the Northwest Passage. Giovanni da Verrazzano, Jacques Cartier, and a host of followers all sought rivers that would link Atlantic to Pacific waters. While the river passage to India remained at the heart of much North American exploration, strategies designed to probe the continent itself also paid attention to rivers. European empire builders, especially the French, quickly recognized the role of rivers like the St. Lawrence and the Mississippi in an expanding colonial domain. Cartier took pains to inform Francis I "of the richness of the great river [St. Lawrence], which flows through and waters the midst of these lands, which is without comparison the largest river that is known to have ever been seen."[4] French explorers, traders, soldiers, and missionaries all shaped their enterprises to the courses of such imperial rivers.[5]

In Anglo-America the tradition of rivers, Eden, and empire found a congenial home in Virginia. From its earliest beginnings, the colony nurtured dreams about waterways heading west to the sunset. Late in the year 1606, as final preparations were underway for the first English voyage to what became Jamestown, the noted geographer and imperial promoter Richard Hakluyt set down his thoughts on what London Company employees might find at America's edge. Hakluyt and other Elizabethan expansionists were of two minds about America. No matter how fascinated they were with the material and imperial rewards the continent promised, they could not shake free from the dream of a passage to the Pacific. It was that obsession with the Pacific—"the Other Sea"—that dominated Hakluyt's thinking about rivers. He suggested company agents locate their post on a navigable river. But no ordinary waterway would do. The geographer urged English explorers to "make Choise of that which bendeth most towards the Northwest for that way shall You soonest find the Other Sea."[6] Standing by themselves, those words could have led English adventurers to think they might find a river canal across the country. But Hakluyt's conception of continental river systems was far more sophisticated. Travelers bound up the great river—a river Hakluyt was certain they would find—were directed to learn if the stream's headwaters were in mountainous terrain. A source of that kind would surely complicate finding a path to the Pacific. But, explained the geographer, "if it be out of any Lake the passage to the Other Sea will be the more Easy." Prefiguring Jefferson's speculations about the symmetrical geography of North American landforms and rivers, Hakluyt insisted that "it was Like Enough that Out of the same Lake you shall find Some Spring which run the Contrary way toward the East India Sea."[7]

Hakluyt's vision of rivers running east and west from a common source became the geographic foundation for generations of Virginia explorers and adventurers. John Smith speculated about a passage to "the back sea" while paddling up the Chickahominy.[8] The Virginia river exploration tradition grew in the middle decades of the seventeenth century with the travels of Edward Bland, Abraham Wood, and John Lederer. Conjectural geography gave impetus to such journeys and reported on discoveries both real and imaginary. And in all of this rivers played a central role. When *A Perfect Description of Virginia* appeared in London in 1649, its anonymous author claimed that just beyond the mountains were "great rivers that run into a great sea." When colonial promoter Edward Williams published his *Virgo Triumphans*, illusion became unquestioned reality. "What opulency does China teeme with," asked Williams, "which shall not be made our owne by the Midwifry of this vital passage?"[9]

Virginia's dreams of western empire grew grander and more seductive in the eighteenth century, thanks in large part to struggles against the French and their native allies. The Ohio country south and west of the Great Lakes promised wealth as well as access to the continent's mightiest rivers. The Mississippi and the Missouri offered the prospect of a greater Virginia, one that might fulfill the hopes of Richard Hakluyt. James Maury, schoolmaster and sometime tutor to Thomas Jefferson, was one of those Virginians caught up in the wonder of countries beyond the Blue Ridge. In a series of letters written to relatives in England in the mid-1750s, he neatly summarized all the speculative talk rattling through Williamsburg taverns and plantation houses. "Whoever takes control of the Ohio and the Lakes," predicted Maury, "will become sole and absolute lord of America."[10] But Maury had more on his mind than one river and the Great Lakes. Hakluyt's conception of symmetrical continental geography, and especially the role of rivers, got expanded treatment at the schoolmaster's hands. Because these geographic images became the core of Jefferson's own conjectural geography about the West and its rivers, Maury's words command special attention:

> When it is considered how far the eastern branches of that immense river, Mississippi, extend eastward, and how near they come to the navigable, or rather canoeable parts of the rivers which empty themselves into the sea that washes our shores to the east, it seems highly probable that its western branches reach as far the other way, and make as near approaches to rivers which empty themselves into the ocean west of us, the Pacific Ocean, across which a short and easy communication, short in comparison with the present route thither, opens itself to the navigator from that shore of the continent unto the Eastern Indies.[11]

Two years after putting those conjectures on paper, Maury became tutor to the young Thomas Jefferson. The impressionable student might have heard his teacher talk about riverways to the Pacific. There may have been asides revealing at least one abortive Virginia expedition up the Missouri to find the passage to India. It is more likely that Jefferson learned lessons about the destiny of a greater Virginia beyond the mountains. But these seeds would take a long time to sprout and flower. Like most Virginians, Jefferson was primarily interested in the Atlantic world. The Pacific and a distant West may have been promising but it was a remote promise at best.

That Atlantic world had markets at its center, markets for the produce of Virginia's farms and plantations. An expanding Virginia demanded an efficient internal transportation system, one that could move heavy commodities over long distances at low cost. Virginians of all ranks and orders were convinced that a water system—one employing existing rivers and new canals—was the answer. Whatever Jefferson's philosophical worries about the relationship between commerce, private vice, and public virtue, he fully embraced the market system. As he once wrote to a European correspondent, "our people have a decided taste for navigation and commerce."[12] It was a taste not to be denied.

Before the American Revolution it was the Rivanna River that captured Jefferson's attention. In 1771 he set in motion plans to make that river a navigable waterway. But the Rivanna could never be the kind of great river so deeply fixed in the Virginia imagination. That distinction might only belong to the Potomac, the Ohio, or the Mississippi. Throughout the crucial decade of the 1780s those rivers, especially the Potomac and the Mississippi, occupied much of Jefferson's time and attention. For him and many of his Virginia contemporaries, the Potomac seemed to offer the greatest promise.

Early in 1784 Jefferson began to think carefully about ways Virginia might benefit from a water transportation system centered on the Potomac. A navigable Potomac could tap the riches of the Ohio country, fulfilling the colonial promise of a greater Virginia in the West. Sounding much like Richard Hakluyt and James Maury, Jefferson lectured James Madison on the fundamentals of a river-based imperial geography. "The Ohio, and its branches which head up against the Patomac affords the shortest water communication by 500 miles of any which can ever be got between the Western waters and the Atlantic, and of course promises us almost a monopoly of the Western and Indian trade." Jefferson's abiding fear was that another state—perhaps Pennsylvania or New York—might develop a waterway system ahead of Virginia. "If we do not push this matter immediately," he predicted that rival states would "be beforehand with us and get possession of the commerce."[13] Madison hardly needed Jefferson's words to convince him. Quick to grasp the relationship between market access and land values, Madison calculated that navigation on the James and Potomac rivers would "double the value of half the lands within the commonwealth, will extend its commerce, link with its interests those of the Western States, and lessen the emigration of its Citizens, by enhancing the profitableness of situations which they now desert in search of better."[14]

While both Jefferson and Madison agreed that the Potomac project was essential for Virginia's economic and political well being, neither wanted to direct so ambitious an enterprise. Jefferson hoped that George Washington would lend his organizational skills and considerable prestige to the venture. And Washington did believe the undertaking to be a worthy one. "I foresee," he observed, "such extensive political consequences depending on the navigation of these two rivers and communicating them by short and easy roads with the waters of the Western Territory."[15] Knowing Washington's interest, Jefferson moved quickly to propose him as the project's director. The father of the nation would become the father of Virginia's waterway empire. In mid-March 1784 Jefferson sent Washington what amounted to an unofficial state paper on the Potomac and Virginia's western future. Jefferson began by accepting the obvious—that "all the world is becoming commercial." Whatever the consequences of such a spirit, to deny the power of that impulse was to court political impotence and economic ruin. Markets and transportation networks, what Jefferson called "this modern source of wealth and power," needed to be turned to Virginia's benefit. In the 1780s Jefferson's geography of empire was bounded by three rivers—the Potomac, the Hudson, and the Mississippi. As he explained it to Washington, the Mississippi would always be the main channel for agricultural and timber products bound out of New Orleans. What remained was "a rivalship between the Hudson and the Patomac for the residue of the commerce of all the country Westward of Lake Erie, on the waters of the lakes, of the Ohio and upper parts of the Missisipi." Comparing mileages and portages, Jefferson played fast and loose with figures to assert that the Potomac route was dramatically shorter and less demanding. In a flight of rhetorical fancy, he claimed that "Nature has declared in favour of the Patomac, and through that channel offers to pour into our lap the whole commerce of the Western world."[16]

For Jefferson, America always seemed to be Virginia writ large. What the Potomac might be for Virginia, the Mississippi could accomplish for the young republic. Empire, expansion, commerce, and union—all issues that embroiled Atlantic nations at the end of the eighteenth century—came together along the banks of the Mississippi. At the end of the American Revolution, Spain and the United States were uneasy allies, bound by a common enemy but deeply suspicious about each other's continental ambitions. As Spanish officials saw it, the United States was an aggressive neighbor bent on invading the lands of His Most Catholic Majesty. Viceroy Manuel Antonio Florez was convinced that the newly independent American states would soon spill over the Mississippi and "carry out the design of finding a safe port on the Pacific."[17] Spanish fears of an imperialist invasion were matched by American nightmares of subversion and encirclement.

Nowhere did that nightmare take on more fearsome proportions then in the settlements of Kentucky and Tennessee. Farmers and merchants employed the Mississippi as the principal means for getting their products to European and West Indian markets. Regional and perhaps even national economic growth depended on free navigation and the right of deposit at New Orleans. The Mississippi Question had a political aspect far more dangerous than its economic dimension. Some in Kentucky and Tennessee argued that if the Confederation government could not negotiate a satisfactory treaty with Spain, the western states should become part of the Spanish empire. The Spanish decision in 1784 to close the lower Mississippi to American traffic and the confused negotiations the next year between John Jay and Spanish ambassador Diego de Gardoqui deepened the crisis. John Brown, a prominent Kentucky politician, put the whole matter to Jefferson in a pointed note. "The ill-advised attempt to cede the navigation of that River has laid the foundation for the dismemberment of the American Empire by destroying the confidence of the people in the Western Country in the Justice of the Union and by inducing them to dispair of obtaining possession of the Right by means of any other exertions than their own."[18]

Even before becoming Secretary of State in 1790, Jefferson had expressed his views on the Mississippi Question. While the economic rewards that flowed through river channels were not to be slighted, Jefferson increasingly thought about rivers in political terms. Rivers might advance the cause of empire while linking backcountry outposts to distant centers of power. "I will venture to say," he wrote to Madison, "that the act which abandons the navigation of the Mississippi is an act of separation between the Eastern and Western country. It is a relinquishment of five parts of eight of the territory of the United States, an abandonment of the fairest subject for the paiment of our public debts, and the chaining those debts on our necks in perpetuum."[19]

Some months after taking his place in Washington's administration, Jefferson drafted a comprehensive policy document on the Mississippi

Question. With war between Spain and England seemingly days or weeks away, the Secretary of State was certain that Spanish officials would be eager to meet with American negotiator William Carmichael. Jefferson's directions to Carmichael reveal just how deeply he had thought about rivers and their role in an American empire. He insisted that the United States had a right to navigation on the Mississippi by both treaty and Nature. Written law and the higher Law of Nature validated that right. This was no abstract "right" to be defended in polite conversation. Jefferson was convinced that transit on the river was fundamental for the political survival of the American nation.[20]

In the two decades after Independence, Thomas Jefferson considered American rivers by means of private letters and public papers. But nowhere did those rivers get more systematic and even poetic treatment than in *Notes on the State of Virginia*. Written in 1780 as a response to a questionnaire from François Marbois, the *Notes* became an armchair exploration of Virginia. And because Virginia was always another way to say America, Jefferson indirectly took on the larger task of charting the destiny of the republic's rivers. Chapter Two in *Notes* provides a detailed list of Virginia's rivers. Scanning that list some two hundred years after Jefferson composed it, two things strike the modern reader. First is the yardstick by which each river was judged. And Jefferson did not merely describe rivers; he judged them. The Enlightenment sensibility calculated nature not by measures of beauty and the picturesque. While Jefferson and his contemporaries were fully capable of appreciating Nature and the Beautiful, such concerns were quite secondary. What mattered, especially in the case of rivers, was the Useful. Nature's beauty was to be found in Nature's utility. When Jefferson applied that standard to rivers, the unit of measure was navigability. Rivers were important and worthy of attention in proportion to their capacity to carry the burdens of commerce. Jefferson assumed that western rivers would have the same kinds of channels and water flows as eastern waterways. The second chapter of *Notes* amounts to an annotated list of rivers and the key annotation is always a comment on navigation. Rivers like the James and the Potomac got Jefferson's approval while the Little Miami of the Ohio was dismissed with a curt "affords no navigation."[21] The focus on navigation reflected the practical concerns of tidewater tobacco planters. But Jefferson's navigation commentaries went well beyond tobacco and a plantation economy. By the 1780s he believed that rivers would be the primary avenues for expansion into the Ohio country and beyond. Empire would follow a water trail; commerce could be a national unifying force. *Notes on the State of Virginia* proposes a river geography, an empire of water courses.

In that imperial geography, two rivers dominated the landscape. Jefferson certainly recognized the Mississippi as "one of the principal channels of future commerce of the country westward of the Alleghaney."[22] But it was the Missouri and its westward course that increasingly captured his attention and imagination. "The Missouri is," so Jefferson wrote, "the principal river, contributing more to the common stream than does the Mississippi." Drawing on images that had been part of the Virginia geographic tradition since Hakluyt and Smith, Jefferson confidently put the Missouri at the center of a passage to the Pacific. He speculated that the Missouri's rapid current meant the river had its headwaters at a high elevation. From unnamed St. Louis merchant sources Jefferson was led to believe that the Missouri ran some two thousand miles inland to its remote mountain springs. Beyond the Missouri was the River of the West, the Ouragon, a river Jefferson would later know as the Columbia. He envisioned the Missouri as not only the gateway to the Pacific but as the prime access route into the Southwest. In the 1780s Spain loomed large as a powerful continental rival. Some maps showed the Missouri taking its great bend as a hairpin turn and then running straight toward Spanish New Mexico. Jefferson estimated that the distance from the mouth of the Ohio to Santa Fe was about one thousand miles, or forty travel days. More important, he thought that the Missouri was at some point fairly close to the elusive Rio Norte and its course toward Santa Fe. Jefferson's image of the Southwest was a tangle of rivers, cities, and mines. The geography of the Missouri and its connections may have been fuzzy in places, but the message was clear. The Missouri was the river route of empire, promising a way west and a way to link West to East.[23]

Notes on the State of Virginia was as clear a statement on rivers and theoretical geography as Jefferson would make for the rest of the decade. Yet the ideas contained in those pages did not mean that he was ready or able to launch exploring parties into the West. In the 1780s Jefferson was still an Atlantic man with a European agenda. But a series of events—interest in the French Lapérouse Expedition to the Pacific, acquaintance with the eccentric adventurer John Ledyard, and growing concern about an Anglo-Canadian presence in the Pacific Northwest—prompted Jefferson to think again about the rivers of empire. Sometime in 1792 he met the French naturalist André Michaux. Michaux had spent some years in eastern North America, botanizing and establishing experimental gardens. By 1791 he seemed ready to return to France. For reasons that are now not clear, Michaux stayed in the United States and in 1792 brought the American Philosophical Society a fascinating proposal. The botanist wanted the

Society to fund a transcontinental trek to the Pacific. What Michaux suggested—an expedition up the Missouri, across the Rockies, and on to the Pacific—was hardly a new exploration strategy. Similar schemes were the common talk in St. Louis and Montreal merchant houses. But in this case, Michaux's ideas fit neatly with Jefferson's own conception of western river systems. By early December 1792 Jefferson was fondly calling Michaux "our South-sea adventurer."²⁴

In the first weeks of 1793 Jefferson became deeply involved in planning the Michaux expedition. As vice-president of the American Philosophical Society, he took the lead in raising funds for the journey. But his real contribution was not financial but intellectual. Jefferson's wide reading in exploration literature taught him that discovery and exploration were carefully programmed inquiries, not aimless hunts for ill-defined treasures. Armed with precise instructions, explorers went in search of places and things already defined. At the end of April 1793 Jefferson sent Michaux detailed directions for the proposed journey. After giving his explorer orders about recording various aspects of the western landscape and cultures, Jefferson turned his attention to the route. The theories and conjectures in *Notes on the State of Virginia* now stood some chance of being tested. What Jefferson wrote summarized several generations of speculation. "As a channel of communication between these states and the Pacific ocean, the Missouri, so far as it extends, presents itself under circumstances of unquestioned preference." In Jefferson's mental geography the Missouri's headwaters were somehow connected to another river—probably the Great River of the West—bound for the Pacific. "It would seem," so he wrote to Michaux, "by the latest maps as if a river called Oregon interlocked with the Missouri."²⁵ Jefferson's river highway was now complete. It remained only for travelers to follow its course and mark its currents.

Despite Jefferson's best efforts, the Michaux expedition failed. Caught up in the western intrigues of Citizen Genet, the erstwhile "South-sea adventurer" abandoned Pacific ambitions and eventually left for France in 1796. As fortune had it, the 1790s proved to be a Canadian decade on the rivers of the West. It was the age of Alexander Mackenzie and David Thompson. Missouri and Columbia river passages edged away from Jefferson as the Mississippi and Spain demanded more attention.

It was not until the summer of 1802 that now-president Thomas Jefferson was pushed to think again about western waterways. Summers at Monticello were always a time to escape the oppressive heat and incessant political chatter of the Federal City. Nothing was a more welcome escape than reading and Jefferson asked his New York bookseller to send along a copy of

Alexander Mackenzie's recently published *Voyages from Montreal.* Jefferson also wanted a copy of Aaron Arrowsmith's newest map of North America, a map that promised to depict "all the new discoveries in the Interior Parts." Most of Mackenzie's book was a dreary recounting of his 1789 and 1792–93 expeditions. But it was his imperial prophecies at the end of the volume that captured Jefferson's attention. Here Mackenzie sketched out an impressive plan for British domination of the West. Rivers—especially the Columbia—were at the heart of that plan. Mackenzie made the role of the Columbia clear when he wrote the following:

> But whatever course may be taken from the Atlantic, the Columbia is the line of communication from the Pacific Ocean, pointed out by nature, as it is the only navigable river in the whole extent of Vancouver's minute survey of that coast: its banks also form the first level country in all the Southern extent of continual coast from Cook's entry, and, consequently, the most Northern situation fit for colonization, and suitable to the residence of a civilized people.[26]

Mackenzie's Columbia promised not only a fur trade empire but the beginnings of permanent Euro-American settlement. That was a challenge Jefferson could not afford to ignore.

By the fall of 1802 the president was busy fashioning what would become the Lewis and Clark expedition. Warned by Secretary of the Treasury Albert Gallatin that any plans for western exploration would meet stiff Federalist opposition, Jefferson sent Congress a confidential appropriation message. That message gave the president his first opportunity to describe a large-scale, river-based trade system, one aimed at defeating any Anglo-Canadian rival. Jefferson argued that Mackenzie's northern route to the Pacific would be hampered by demanding portages and harsh winter conditions. On the other hand, the Missouri ran through what he optimistically characterized as "a moderate climate." More important, the Missouri was part of an almost uninterrupted transcontinental waterway system. "According to the best accounts," Jefferson reported, the Missouri offered "a continued navigation from its sources and, possibly with a single portage, from the Western ocean, and finding to the Atlantic a choice of channels through the Illinois or Wabash, the Lakes and Hudson, through the Ohio and Susquehanna or Potomac or James rivers, and through the Tennessee and Savannah rivers."[27] This litany of rivers was more than a catalogue of American waterways. It was Jefferson's way of subduing nature, making its courses and currents serve the purposes of a growing republic.

Soon after sending his thoughts on rivers and commercial empire to Congress, Jefferson received two letters that even more sharply focused his thinking about waterways and expansion. Albert Gallatin's interests and abilities went far beyond those usually required for a treasury official. Gallatin read widely in geography, ethnography, linguistics, and the natural sciences. In early April 1803, as Jefferson was beginning to flesh out details for an expedition to the Pacific, Gallatin wrote the president a remarkable letter— remarkable for its grasp of imperial geography and prophetic vision of an expanding nation. "The future destinies of the Missouri country are of vast importance to the United States, it being perhaps the only large tract of country, and certainly the first which lying out of the boundaries of the Union will be settled by the people of the U. States." The exploration of western rivers was a "grand object" going well beyond fur trade competition. As Gallatin saw it, American explorers were pushing up the Missouri "to ascertain whether from its extent and fertility that country is susceptible of a large population, in the same manner as the corresponding tract on the Ohio."[28]

Gallatin's vision of a settlement empire was given a larger context in a letter from naturalist Bernard Lacépède. His observations confirmed Jefferson's own conception of both western geography and the role of rivers in territorial expansion. "If your nation," wrote Lacépède, "could establish an easy communication route by river, canal and short portages, between New Yorck, for example, and the town which would be built at the mouth of the Columbia, what a route that would be for trade from Europe, from Asia, and from America, whose northern products would arrive at this route by the Great Lakes and the upper Mississippi, while the southern products of the New World would arrive there by the Lower Mississippi and by the Rio Norte of New Mexico, the source of which is near the 40th parallel." Like Jefferson, Lacépède linked water highways to issues well beyond the daily routines of profit and loss. Commerce was a civilizing force, a power that tamed avarice and directed it in useful channels. "What greater means," declared Lacépède, "to civilization than these new communication routes."[29]

By the time Jefferson began to write exploring instructions for Meriwether Lewis, he had thought long and hard about the meaning of rivers. The Missouri was the master river for American expansion. It was empire's plain path. Tributaries were important in relation to the main stem of the Missouri. Drafted toward the end of June 1803, instructions for Lewis summed up years of thinking about rivers and western geography. "The object of your mission," wrote Jefferson, "is to explore the Missouri river, and such principal stream of it, as, by it's course and communication with the waters of the Pacific ocean, whether the Columbia, Oregan, Colorado or any other river may offer the most direct and practicable water communication across the continent for the purposes of commerce."[30] The word *commerce* has often been interpreted in this context to mean the fur trade. It is clear that Jefferson meant much more than the trade in peltries. American farmers would not be willing to settle in the western lands unless there was some means to transport agricultural goods to market. Jefferson's West promised continued vitality to the republic and that vitality depended on the incentives of commerce and inexpensive water transportation. When Lewis suggested a side trip toward Santa Fe before the main journey up the Missouri, Jefferson sharply reminded the captain of his primary task. "The object of your mission is single, the direct water communication from sea to sea formed by the bed of the Missouri and perhaps the Oregon."[31]

While Lewis's mission was "single," Jefferson was not about to ignore other western rivers. Once the process of ratifying the Louisiana Purchase treaty was underway, the president began to create a large-scale plan for the exploration of western rivers. "I have proposed in conversation," he explained to Lewis, "that Congress shall appropriate 10 or 12000 D. for exploring the principal waters of the Mississippi and the Missouri. In that case I should send a party up the Red river to its head, then to cross over to the head of the Arcansa, and come down that. A 2d. party for the Pani and Padocua rivers, and a 3d. perhaps for the Moingona and St. Peters."[32] The Red and Arkansas rivers were especially important in light of simmering boundary disputes with Spain. In April 1804 Jefferson sent Thomas Freeman instructions for the exploration of those rivers. These directions were freely adapted from the ones drafted for Lewis a year earlier.[33]

Jefferson's expectations about western rivers were built not only on a faulty geography but on a set of fantasies about the West as a physical setting. Jefferson and his explorers envisioned a West cut through with rivers longer and deeper than any in the East. One French observer captured that sense of western grandness when he wrote that "each step one takes from East to West, the size of all objects increases ten-fold in volume."[34] Such enthusiasm was bound to collide with harsh reality, producing along the way both more fantasy and bitter disappointment. The Freeman-Custis Red River expedition of 1806 was stopped by inadequate planning, low water, and the presence of armed Spanish forces. Jefferson's cherished dream of a Missouri-Columbia passage across the continent was mortally wounded at Lemhi Pass in August 1805 when Lewis and Clark found not Pacific waters but the seemingly endless Bitterroot Mountains. Lewis wrote an obituary for that part of Jefferson's geographic dream in September 1806 when the expedition returned to St. Louis. "We view this passage across the Continent as affording immence advantages for the fur trade, but fear that the advantages which it offers as a communication for the productions of the East Indies to the United States and thence to Europe will never be found equal on an extensive scale to that by way of the Cape of Good Hope."[35] Navigability—the measure of utility in Jefferson's river world—had led him astray in the West. Western rivers were not like those in the East. In coming years the greatest irony was that the nearly impassable Platte River proved the route for both wagons and rails.

Jefferson and his contemporaries often talked about rivers as "communications," passages that could spread wealth and knowledge. Writing in the 1790s, inventor and promoter Robert Fulton expressed the Enlightenment optimism that nourished such beliefs. "An easy communication," he explained, "brings remote parts into nearer alliance, combines the exertions of men, distributes their labours through a variety of channels, and spreads with greater regularity the blessings of life."[36] Jefferson expected western rivers to communicate many things. They might carry messages of expansion and parcels of profit. Perhaps more important in his scheme of empire, rivers would carry the message of union and nation. Rivers were to direct the course of empire and yet confine its turbulent currents between banks of Reason and Law. Jefferson imagined rivers enlarging his Empire for Liberty while at the same time imposing order and stability. Those expectations—often contradictory images of growth and order—came through when the president wrote William Dunbar in late May 1805. The task of explorers and their patrons was to "delineate with correctness the great arteries of this great country: those who come after us will extend the ramifications as they become acquainted with them, and fill up the canvas we begin."[37] For Jefferson filling the canvas meant painting river outlines. Once the boundaries had been sketched, the western portrait could be finished. But the realities of western geography were not kind of Jefferson's river drawings. As his explorers learned, dreams of navigation proved illusory. The Platte, the Green, and the Snake were not like the Rivanna, the James, or the Potomac. As fortune had it, the promise of rivers settled on other ways west. Waterways, so much a part of the Virginia tradition, were left behind as a westering nation turned to railways and highways. The western canvas proved to have outlines and boundaries not of water, but of steel and concrete. Expansion and unification—the promise of Jefferson's rivers—came to life along railroad rights-of-way and on the lanes of the Interstate Highway System.

Notes

My thinking about American rivers has been both influenced and challenged by two superb books by John Seelye. *Prophetic Waters: The River in Early American Life and Literature* (New York: Oxford University Press, 1977) and *Beautiful Machine: Rivers and the Republican Plan, 1755–1825* (New York: Oxford University Press, 1991) are essential reading. Donald Worster, *Rivers of Empire: Water, Aridity, and the Growth of the American West* (New York: Pantheon Books, 1985) has given me a sense of the ways Jefferson's thoughts about rivers shaped later public policy decisions. My reading of Jefferson has been made sharper (I hope) thanks to Charles A. Miller, *Jefferson and Nature: An Interpretation* (Baltimore: Johns Hopkins University Press, 1988). All who write about American rivers work in the shadow of Samuel Langhorne Clemens. I gratefully acknowledge my debt to Mark Twain and *Life on the Mississippi.*

1. Thomas Jefferson, "A Memorandum (Services to My Country)," Merrill D. Peterson, ed., *Thomas Jefferson: Writings* (New York: Library of America, 1984), 702; "Project for Making the Rivanna River Navigable, 1771," Julian Boyd, et. al., eds., *Papers of Thomas Jefferson*, 28 vols. to date (Princeton: Princeton University Press, 1950–), 1: 87–88. Hereafter cited as TJP.

2. Genesis 2: 10.

3. J. M. Cohen, trans., *The Four Voyages of Christopher Columbus* (Baltimore: Penguin Books, 1969), 222.

4. David B. Quinn, ed., *New American World: A Documentary History of North America to 1612*, 5 vols. (New York: Arno Press, 1979), 1: 305.

5. Andrew Hill Clark, "The Conceptions of Empires of the St. Lawrence and the Mississippi," *American Review of Canadian Studies* 5 (1975): 4–27.

6. Richard Hakluyt, "Instructions given by way of advice," in Philip L. Barbour, ed., *The Jamestown Voyages under the First Charter 1606–1609*, 2 vols. (Cambridge, England: Hakluyt Society, 1969), 1: 49.

7. Ibid., 1: 51.

8. John Smith, "A True Relation," in ibid., 1: 186.

9. Quotations from *A Perfect Description of Virginia* and *Virgo Triumphans* are in William P. Cumming, et. al., *The Exploration of North America, 1630–1776* (New York: G. P. Putnam, 1974), 82–83.

10. James Maury in Seelye, *Beautiful Machine*, 36.

11. Ibid., 38.

12. Jefferson to G. K. van Hogendorp, Paris, 13 October 1785, TJP, 8: 633.
13. Jefferson to Madison, Annapolis, 20 February 1784, TJP, 6: 548.
14. Madison to Jefferson, Richmond, 9 January 1785, TJP, 7: 592.
15. Washington to Jefferson, Mt. Vernon, 25 February 1785, TJP, 8: 4.
16. Jefferson to Washington, Annapolis, 15 March 1784, TJP, 7: 26.
17. William R. Manning, "The Nootka Sound Controversy," *Annual Report* of the American Historical Association for the Year 1904 (Washington, D.C.: Government Printing Office, 1905), 302.
18. John Brown to Jefferson, New York, 10 August 1788, TJP, 13: 494. The larger context is skillfully laid out in Reginald Horsman, *The Diplomacy of the New Republic 1776–1815* (Arlington Heights, Ill.: Harlan Davidson, 1985), ch. 1.
19. Jefferson to Madison, Paris, 30 January 1787, TJP, 11: 93.
20. Jefferson, "Outline of Policy on the Mississippi Question, 2 August 1790," TJP, 17: 113–16. See also Jefferson's "Report on Negotiations with Spain, 18 March 1792," TJP, 23: 296–312.
21. Thomas Jefferson, *Notes on the State of Virginia*, William Peden, ed. (Chapel Hill: University of North Carolina Press, 1954), 13.
22. Ibid., 7.
23. Ibid., 8–9.
24. Jefferson to Benjamin Smith Barton, Philadelphia, 2 December 1792, TJP, 24: 687.
25. Jefferson to Michaux, Philadelphia, 30 April 1793, Donald Jackson, ed., *The Letters of the Lewis and Clark Expedition with Related Documents 1783–1854*, 2nd ed., 2 vols. (Urbana: University of Illinois Press, 1978), 2: 669–72.
26. W. Kaye Lamb, ed., *The Journals and Letters of Sir Alexander Mackenzie* (Cambridge, England: Hakluyt Society, 1970), 417.
27. Jefferson, "Confidential Message to Congress, 18 January 1803," Jackson, ed., *Letters*, 1: 12–13.
28. Gallatin to Jefferson, Washington, 13 April 1803, ibid., 1: 33.
29. Lacépède to Jefferson, 13 May 1803, ibid., 1: 47.
30. Jefferson to Lewis, Washington, 20 June 1803, ibid., 1: 62.
31. Jefferson to Lewis, Washington, 16 November 1803, ibid., 1: 137.
32. Ibid.
33. Jefferson to Thomas Freeman, Monticello, 14 April 1804, Dan L. Flores, ed., *Jefferson and Southwestern Exploration: The Freeman and Custis Accounts of the Red River Expedition of 1806* (Norman: University of Oklahoma Press, 1984), 320–25.

34. Louis Vilemont to Minister, Sedan, France, 6 June 1802, A. P. Nasatir, ed., *Before Lewis and Clark: Documents Illustrating the History of the Missouri, 1785–1804,* 2 vols. (St. Louis: St. Louis Documents Foundation, 1952), 2: 699.

35. Lewis to Jefferson, St. Louis, 23 September 1806, Jackson, ed., *Letters,* 1: 321.

36. Robert Fulton, *A Treatise on the Improvement of Canal Navigation* (London, 1796) in Seelye, *Beautiful Machine,* 231.

37. Jefferson to Dunbar, Washington, 25 May 1805, Jackson, ed., *Letters,* 1: 245.

T W O

Lewis and Clark
in the Age(s) of Exploration

On April 7, 1805—the day the Corps of Discovery left Fort Mandan for points West—Meriwether Lewis entered an intriguing, revealing note in his journal. The words are so compelling, so resonant, that they deserve special attention. Surveying the expedition's collection of canoes and perogues, Lewis wrote: "This little fleet altho' not quite so rispectable as those of Columbus or Captain Cook were still viewed by us with as much pleasure as those deservedly famed adventurers ever beheld theirs."[1]

We could say that this was whistling in the dark, some bold words about an uncertain journey into suspect terrain. To be even less charitable about it, we might hear Lewis's words as brag talk—a young, still-untested American adventurer presumptuously putting himself in company with the idols of the age. And Lewis was surely capable of such posturing, both in person and in his journal. But we might also read Lewis's words another way. Perhaps we should hear them as Lewis's appreciation for his place in the larger history of American geographic exploration. On that day in early April Lewis had "a sense of history," something like a shock of recognition.

It should come as no shock that Lewis invoked two emblematic names—Christopher Columbus and James Cook. Columbus and the Atlantic; Cook and the Pacific. And perhaps for the country in between, Lewis could reserve that place for himself and Thomas Jefferson's Corps of Discovery. As we consider the Lewis and Clark journey, it might help if we take Lewis's words quite seriously. He meant to place his voyage in some larger context. And the frame he chose—Columbus and Cook—was both obvious and appropriate. Naming them, Lewis acknowledged what he had inherited and what might be his place in that complicated, often troubled legacy.

Think of it this way: Lewis, Clark, Jefferson, and their whole exploration enterprise were recipients of a trust, inheritors of a rich, intricate, and morally complex set of traditions. Those exploration traditions ring with names like Marco Polo, Martin Frobisher, Henry Hudson, and the shadowy John Day. The Lewis and Clark Expedition was not a beginning but a continuation, not a finale but one more act in a still-unfinished drama. Jefferson and his travelers inherited the legacies of Columbus and Cook. So we might ask—what was that inheritance? What ideas, conceptions, notions, illusions, fantasies, sound practices, and just plain silliness did Columbus and Cook bequeath to a visionary American president and two Army officers? Keep in mind as we explore these Last Wills and Testaments that no one—neither Lewis and Clark nor Jefferson—could have known all the subtleties and nuances in that inheritance.

Washington Irving did not publish his epic, mythmaking biography of Christopher Columbus until 1828, but Lewis and Clark and their contemporaries already held Columbus in the greatest reverence. By the time Lewis linked himself to the Great Navigator, the name Columbus pointed not so much to one historical person as to an entire, extended generation of sailors, explorers, cartographers, and empire builders. The Columbus generation included John Cabot, his son Sebastian, Giovanni da Verrazzano, Jacques Cartier, and the irrepressible Sir Humphry Gilbert. Their dreams, and the voyages that sprang from them, were bound together by a shared set of ideas and illusions, strategies and expectations. The Lewis and Clark Expedition drew on all of that for inspiration, guidance, and perhaps a sense of historical legitimacy as well.

We might consider three distinct features of the Columbus generation that shaped the way the Corps of Discovery thought about itself and its mission.

FIRST: Threading its way through the whole Lewis and Clark enterprise is one compelling idea, an illusion with a magnetism that defies all laws of reason and physics. When Jefferson commanded his captains to find "the most direct and practicable water communication across this continent for the purposes of commerce," he was repeating a geographic vocabulary already centuries old.[2] This was the deathless dream—the belief that there had to be some kind of navigable water highway through barrier America. In the first years of the sixteenth century it was Sebastian Cabot who gave initial shape to what others soon called the Northwest Passage. The promise of the passage was the fulfillment of the Columbus dream—a way across the western sea to India and China. Later, the passage took on many shapes and locations. Some imagined it as an open-water connection in the Arctic; others fancied rivers like the St. Lawrence, the Hudson, or even the

Missouri as trans-continental passages. And in *Leaves of Grass*, poet Walt Whitman gave the idea lyrical expression in his poem "Passage to India." Few geographic fantasies have proved so durable. Imagination and desire joined hands in the quest for the ever-elusive highway through America. The passage was there, somewhere, because it had to be. The passage became an article of faith in the catechism of optimism. Sailing off the coast of the Carolina Outer Banks in 1524, Giovanni da Verrazzano was certain he glimpsed the Pacific Ocean glittering in the western distance. The passage would not be hard and the "happy shores of Cathay" seemed but a motion away. Some three hundred years later and half a continent away, Meriwether Lewis reached the headwaters of the Missouri River, paused at the crest of Lemhi Pass on the Continental Divide, and fully expected to see waters leading directly to the Pacific Ocean. So it was with imagination and illusion; so it is with legacy and inheritance.

SECOND: The exploration tradition fashioned by the Columbus generation surely contained more than its fair share of illusion and fantasy. But at the same time that heritage included a large measure of sound experience and practical advice. Captains haunted by dreams of China beyond Carolina still kept a weather eye, still respected the ancient wisdom possessed by all seafarers. The voyages of Cabot and Cartier, Verrazzano and Estevão Gómes all offered reliable lessons in the art of discovery, the daily routines of travel and exploration.

The first of those lessons taught the necessity for careful planning. In the nineteenth century, explorers were cast as daring, self-sacrificing, and heroic. And we continue—at least in popular culture—to depict explorers as romantic adventurers, stumbling around in the unknown dark, traveling more by random and chance than by knowledge and experience. But whatever goal they had in mind, explorers bound for or into America did so with the benefit of planning. Goals were defined, authorities consulted, and modes of transport selected. Mental journeys of preparation always preceded physical ventures. This was a lesson not lost on Thomas Jefferson. As he studied accounts of earlier voyages, the message was unmistakable. Purpose and planning were expedition fundamentals, fundamentals exemplified by the Columbus generation.

The second lesson was closely linked to the first. With our romantic passion for the solitary hero it is deceptively simple to imagine explorers as somehow going it alone. The fantasy of solitary achievement is everywhere. We read a book and think only of the author; we watch a film, praise the actors and the director, and then leave before the credits roll. Thomas Jefferson knew better, thanks in large part to the inheritance from the

Columbus generation. Jefferson understood and appreciated the necessity for organization—organization of both the traveling company itself and of those who stayed behind. It was the distinguished exploration scholar Donald Jackson who put it best: "It is no longer useful to think of the Lewis and Clark Expedition as the personal story of two men. Their journey was an enterprise of many aims and a product of many minds."[3]

We see the Corps of Discovery making its way from Atlantic to Pacific waters. What is invisible but ever-present is a much larger body—a whole company of men and women without whose minds and muscles the journey simply would not have happened. We might pause to remember the work of seamstress Matilda Chapman, tinmaker Thomas Passmore, and fishing tackle dealer George Lawton—all members of the Philadelphia trade and craft community. And there were similar trade and craft communities among native people from the Mandan villages to the Clatsop settlement on the very edge of the Pacific. *Infrastructure* is a very modern word—surely not one in Jefferson's vocabulary. But as an exploration patron and planner, he readily acknowledged voyages of discovery as large-scale and intensely planned human enterprises with some of their most important actors either off-stage or in the orchestra pit.

And we should not be so naive as to think that organization could be effective without money. In 1784, after Jefferson asked George Rogers Clark (William's older brother) to consider leading an expedition to the Pacific, George Rogers went straight to the heart of the matter. Who would pay for such a hazardous, speculative journey? George Rogers had made such a journey into the Illinois Country during the American Revolution and now his life had been blighted by expedition debts—debts shrugged off by successive Virginia governors and politicians including Jefferson himself. More than anyone else, George Rogers knew that organized exploration could not be the work of a single individual. His answer was the answer of the Columbus generation and his own time as well. The nation-state—in this case the United States Congress—seemed obvious to George Rogers even three years before the drafting of the federal Constitution. And nearly twenty years later when William Clark accepted Meriwether Lewis's invitation to join the Corps of Discovery, he asked and answered the same question: who will pay? And the answer was the same. It would be government, not some private trading company, not some wealthy individual, not even some missionary church in search of souls to save. Both Clarks recognized a fundamental lesson from the Columbus generation. Only nation-states had pockets deep enough, treasuries rich enough to fund exploration of distant places. Columbus had Ferdinand and Isabella; Cabot had Henry VII;

Cartier had Francis I. Exploration was an affair of state, a matter of national concern. Levi Lincoln, Jefferson's able Attorney General, put it best when he described the Lewis and Clark expedition as "an enterprise of national consequence."[4]

The Columbus generation offered yet a third lesson about the structure of exploration. More than one historian has noticed the striking relationship between the earliest Atlantic voyages of discovery and the spread of printing and printed books in western Europe. It was the seventeenth-century English essayist Sir Francis Bacon who said it best. He observed that printing, gunpowder, and the compass had "changed the appearance and state of the whole world."[5] The compass moved navigation from an art to a science, gunpowder gave conquest almost unimaginable power, and printing expanded the reach and range of knowledge. The voyages of the Columbus generation sailed in an ocean of print. Columbus's key letter describing his travels was first printed in Barcelona in mid-April, 1493— merely a month after he returned from the Caribbean. And in less than six months there were printed translations in Castilian, German, and Italian. In this growing culture of print—this Gutenberg galaxy—explorers found a way both to record and spread their findings. Printed books, pamphlets, and maps provided the vital link between the explorer and those who stayed at home. Print put exploration in an expanding cultural marketplace. And a growing reading public eagerly awaited exploration narratives, both for purposes of commercial information and entertainment. This is not to suggest that in the first century of printing narratives of exploration and travel were suddenly available in large numbers. The early printing houses tended to publish established texts in philosophy, theology, and the ancient classics. But by the end of the sixteenth century, travel narratives were a printer's stock-in-trade. Best known of these was Richard Hakluyt's *Principal Navigations of the English Nation* (1589), a compendium that found an important place in Jefferson's own library. And remember that after Lewis's death in 1809, Clark and Jefferson struggled for five years to get their expedition record into print.

Planning, organization, the support of a state, and the diffusion of knowledge by means of print—all this sounds like the eighteenth-century Enlightenment, or perhaps even our own time. But these aspects of exploration came by way of the Columbus generation, from a time at once medieval and yet Renaissance, at once grounded in the ancient world of Greece and Rome and yet almost modern. And nowhere is that odd, disturbing tension more plain than in the last key feature of the Columbus exploration tradition.

We sometimes talk about exploration in polar terms; not the North or South Poles, but polar opposites. So we hear clichés like: the known and the unknown, the enlightened meets the primitive, the civilized encounters the savage. Meriwether Lewis certainly thought in those terms. On April 7, 1805—the same day that he conjured up the spirits of Columbus and Cook—Lewis characterized his own journey by saying that the Corps of Discovery was "about to penetrate a country . . . on which the foot of civilized man had never trodden."[6]

Lewis's mental image of his footprints as the first on a supposedly virgin land is powerfully evocative, perhaps reminding us of those first astronaut bootprints on the lunar surface. But of course by describing his journey in such terms, Lewis committed an act of historical and cultural erasure. On the same day that he put himself into the collective memory of other European travelers he attempted to rub out the traces of Native American explorers. He summarily erased all the footprints of those who had called the country ahead home long before he came knocking on the western door. Why did he envision exploration in general and his enterprise in particular in such stark, profoundly either/or terms? His was to be the first imprint; all others were dismissed as uncivilized and of no account.

Here the young American was acting out yet another portion of the Columbus generation script. Thinking in dualities, polarities, dichotomies has long been a part of the western, Euro-American intellectual tradition. Mind and body, air and earth, fire and water, perfect good and absolute evil, salvation and damnation; these are all expressions of that polarized world view. Perhaps these couplings represent a fear of ambiguity, the love of secure borders and known boundaries. The earliest European narratives of American exploration all embodied that way of seeing, that way of understanding—or misunderstanding. When applied to the natural world and the native world, this tradition yielded a whole range of powerful and enduring polarities. The original peoples of the Americas were depicted as either children of innocence in a world before the fall or as veritable servants of Satan. So it was with the world of nature as well. American nature was either the Garden of Eden or paradise lost, either (as Lewis put it) "seens of visionary inchantment" or the great American desert.[7] And we continue to hear echoes of this duality when the United States as a political community is described as either the last, best hope of the world or a blot on the conscience of humankind.

Traditions neither live or arrive in tightly sealed containers. We might think of their boundaries as semipermeable membranes. Traditions are always in flux, always changing, always exchanging. The exploration tradition fashioned by the Columbus generation did not reach Thomas Jefferson and Lewis and Clark as a neatly wrapped package, its seals intact over three centuries. Instead, what Columbus and Cabot, Verrazzano and Cartier shaped and experienced came by way of, passed through, and was transformed by the eighteenth-century sensibilities and voyages of figures like James Cook, George Vancouver, and the inestimable Sir Joseph Banks. If Lewis sought identification with Cook, Jefferson would have surely chosen Banks as his model. Banks was president of the Royal Society, Great Britain's foremost scientific body. Perhaps Jefferson drew a parallel between Banks and the Royal Society and his own role with the American Philosophical Society. Banks was a patron of global exploration and an explorer of the South Pacific in his own right. Captain James Cook made three epic voyages of exploration in the Pacific before his death in 1779. But it was Banks who provided the intellectual foundation for those journeys.

When Lewis called up the name of Columbus, he was linking himself to the past. Saying the name Cook connected him to the present, to the contemporary, to the distinctly modern. Lewis, Clark, and Jefferson acted their parts on an exploration stage dominated by the greats of the age—James Cook, George Vancouver, Alejandro Malespina, Jean François Lapérouse. But for global exploration it was the age of Cook and Banks. The memory of Cook's three voyages was still fresh; Cook had been dead only twenty-six years when Lewis wrote his April journal entry. Both Lewis and Clark had some nodding acquaintance with the published reports from Cook's third voyage along the Northwest Coast—ironically a voyage in search of the Northwest Passage. And Sir Joseph Banks—the most influential exploration theorist of the age—was still very much alive. Banks and Jefferson never corresponded directly but they did maintain contact by way of intermediaries like Thomas Paine. And they did share a common interest in the ill-fated explorer John Ledyard. One of Banks' many admirers once called him "the common center of we discoverers."[8] Surely Thomas Jefferson hoped to be that center for his discoverers.

We need to focus our attention on Banks. Captain James Cook was the media star, the darling of the age. There was even a Wedgewood medallion issued in his honor. But Banks was the planner, the strategist, the powerful intelligence that linked Enlightenment philosophies to dreams of empire and the more mundane concerns of ships, sailors, and uncharted waters.

Born in 1743 (the same year as Thomas Jefferson), Joseph Banks grew up in a world of wealth and privilege. A son of the English landed aristocracy and plainly a man of fortune, Banks possessed the leisure and the resources to be both gentleman and naturalist. Predictably, his first love was botany and natural history. That passion broadened over the years to include everything from ethnography to agricultural economics. As president of the Royal Society, virtual director of the Royal Gardens at Kew, and scientific advisor to George III, Banks exercised unparalleled influence both in matters of state and matters of the mind. Banks was a public intellectual long before the likes of Henry Kissinger, George Will, or Doris Kearns Goodwin. We might best consider Banks (and Jefferson for that matter) not as a research scientist but as a scientific entrepreneur much like his seventeenth-century mentor Sir Francis Bacon. Like Bacon, Banks believed that useful knowledge gained by experience and experiment when put in the hands of a benevolent government could improve the condition of all humankind. Such was the creed of the English Enlightenment, and in many ways this became the American tradition as well.

When we look into the Banks-Cook-Enlightenment exploration tradition we can see three influential ideas—ideas that Jefferson admired, accepted, and hoped to employ when he became the common center of the American discoverers.

FIRST: Voyages of discovery and exploration had as their primary goal the acquisition of knowledge. Exploration was not for adventure but for learning, not as an escape from reality but a probing of it. Yet to say that Banks or Jefferson promoted journeys in search of knowledge tells only half the story. As Banks repeatedly insisted, knowledge was valuable only to the extent that it was useful. Knowledge could not be an end in itself. Utility was the yardstick; utility in the service of human society. For example, neither Banks nor Jefferson would have supported an expedition to climb a mountain just because it was there. They would have dismissed such a journey as self-indulgent and romantic nonsense. At its best, exploration aimed at the increase of useful knowledge—knowledge that might enlarge the food supply, expand commercial markets, or increase the security of the nation.

SECOND: Banks and some of his contemporaries believed in the power of a benevolent nation to effect gradual change for the good of all. Banks was comfortable in his faith that the British Empire represented the greatest good for the greatest number. In this perhaps self-righteous, certainly self-serving brand of imperialism, exploration was the prime means for expanding the empire. For Banks, the Cook and Vancouver voyages represented expansion by peaceful, scientific means, not by violence and conquest. In the Banksian scheme of things the explorer was not a warrior or an invader but a friendly botanist, an honest merchant, or even a well-intentioned missionary. The irony in all of this is obvious to us; the self-deception seems plain now. But we need to remember that self-deception is not always clear to the self being deceived.

THIRD: Joseph Banks understood that he was uniquely placed in British public life as an exploration patron. He was of the government, not in the government. He occupied no official office but had the ear of many who did. His social status gave him instant admission into the most influential households, parlors, and coffeehouses. And as president of the Royal Society Banks spoke with great authority. What Banks created and Jefferson sought to emulate was a patron role. Banks envisioned something that went well beyond the familiar conception of a patron as a source of funds or political influence. Instead, he imagined the patron as an enlightened scholar–planner–intermediary, a broker bringing together the worlds of government and science for the benefit of all. It was a role that Thomas Jefferson first found congenial and then quite irresistible.

We should not think of these two exploration traditions as separate threads, each on its own individual spool. Instead, we might stretch our imaginations to envision something woven, a fabric where threads are at once themselves and yet part of something larger. And there is one place we can go to see the ways Thomas Jefferson chose his threads and made his own distinctive design.

In so many ways Jefferson's letter of June 1803 to Lewis represents the synthesis of these two exploration traditions. A recent biographer has described Jefferson as a "textual" president.[9] If the words were right on paper, Jefferson was persuaded that the results would be assured. The attention to detail that he took in the Declaration of Independence can be seen in what became the charter document for all government exploration in the American West for the remainder of the nineteenth century. This key text is the letter that presents Meriwether Lewis with detailed instructions for his coming journey. Reading the letter we cannot help but hear echoes from both the Columbus generation and the age of Cook and Banks. Jefferson was a synthetic thinker, not a strikingly original one like his friend James Madison. Jefferson was at his best when he could pull together bits and pieces of various philosophies and systems, cutting and fitting them to serve his own designs. And how did Jefferson come to know about the visions and voyages of other times and his own? He explained that in one simple, memorable sentence. "I cannot live without books."[10] It was reading—intensive and extensive—in all sorts of travel and exploration accounts that made Jefferson the intellectual patron of western American exploration. And of course it was the power of the presidency that allowed him to move as a patron from thought to action.

What was the Jeffersonian synthesis? What did he take from his predecessors and his contemporaries, reshape for himself, and then hand to Lewis and Clark? That letter of instructions to Lewis tells the story. In it we can discern four distinctive threads from the past, the strands of two traditions now woven into an American one.

FIRST: The very form of Jefferson's letter is revealing. It is at heart a list of questions—questions that range from botany to zoology, from climatology to physiology by way of analytical geography, political theory, and imperial strategy. Those questions are disguised as declarative sentences but they were intended to be read as interrogative ones. Jefferson, Banks, and their contemporaries thought in terms of inquiry. Jefferson loved questions and questionnaires. His only published book, *Notes on the State of Virginia*, was written in response to a series of questions and is arranged in question and answer form. Like Cook and Vancouver, Lewis and Clark were guided by a series of carefully framed questions. What moved explorers from place to place was the power of the question.

SECOND: Reading Jefferson's letter in geographic terms is like taking a crash course in the history of conjectural geography. The mind of Cabot is here; the mind of Cook is here; and most certainly the mind of Sir Joseph Banks is here. Like his contemporaries, Jefferson believed in a balance in nature. The natural world, in all its varied terrain features, was fundamentally symmetrical in construction. In practical terms, this meant that the mountains of the American West simply had to be, in shape and elevation, much like those of the East. If the Appalachians were tree-covered, relatively smooth, and cut through by passes and water-gaps, then the Rockies were sure to be the same. And if the rivers of the east—the Hudson, the Potomac, and the Ohio—were navigable, then certainly western rivers would be open to the benefits of commerce. The face of the earth was not chaotic but well-ordered, not unbalanced but steadied in a kind of symmetrical equilibrium. And through all this danced the dream of a passage from Atlantic to Pacific. Jefferson was captured by that dream—the dream of a passage into his cherished Garden of the West and a passage to the Pacific. The garden and the passage—the scarlet thread that runs back to Columbus and perhaps beyond.

THIRD: Explorers from the Columbus generation to Banks and Cook looked to government, the nation-state. Behind every explorer was someone in the national treasury counting the cash and keeping the books. By the time Banks entered the picture in the 1760s it was well established that exploration on any large scale was of necessity a function of the state. Exploration was financed by the state, manned and led by military or naval personnel, and sent out for reasons of state. Jefferson accepted that gospel but on one crucial point changed it to find his own political ideology. While he had no doubt that government would fund and initiate western exploration, he also believed that the republic would be best served if private individuals and business concerns followed up on what his Corps of Discovery uncovered. Ever wary of centralized power, Jefferson did not want the beneficial results of exploration monopolized by an influential few in government.

FOURTH: When it came to thinking about the purposes of exploration in the grander scheme of things, Jefferson's letter to Lewis is a commentary and an echo—a commentary on the Enlightenment and an echo of so much in the Atlantic intellectual conversation. Here Jefferson and Banks spoke with one voice. Exploration was all about acquiring knowledge—useful knowledge. But they agreed on something else as well, something less apparent and more elusive. Both exploration patrons hoped that journeys of discovery would be forces for national renewal. Banks envisioned exploration in the Pacific as a means to revive the fortunes of the British Empire after the loss of the American colonies in the revolution of 1776. Jefferson—rooted in his hopes for a self-reliant farmer republic—saw exploration as a way to open new lands for agricultural settlement. New lands and new routes would keep Americans out of the industrial cities and forever down on the farm. The exploration of the West might be part of the salvation of the republic.

For a very long time Americans of whatever stripe or color have found it convenient to ignore the past. When the past does intrude we are quick to make it a time for celebration of national genius and accomplishment. The mainstream of our culture is—to the surprise of no one—focused on today and perhaps just a bit obsessed with tomorrow. In our public pronouncements the future has always meant more than the past. We make the past present only in fleeting moments. In America the past is not a presence. But there have been moments—moments of recognition and appreciation. Meriwether Lewis was a brash, brooding, often quite unpleasant young man. He could be both courageous and insufferably arrogant. But on April 7, 1805—when he repeated the names Columbus and Cook—he sensed something about tradition, continuity, about being part of something larger than himself. At least for that moment Lewis recognized his past. But remember that while paying tribute to the footprints of Columbus and Cook, he erased the signs of other explorers and travelers. Acknowledging Columbus and Cook, Lewis neglected Mandan cartographers, Hidatsa travelers, and countless other native adventurers whose footprints were on the land long before his. Perhaps William Clark came closer to recognizing the presence and significance of Native American explorers when he quietly noted that "our information is altogether from Indians collected at different times and entitled to some credit."[11] As we seek to account for the Lewis and Clark Expedition, we need to recall the larger worlds, the deeper times in which all these wayfarers moved. Lewis was surrounded on that April day by a host of invisible explorers and exploration traditions. Thomas Jefferson's Corps of Discovery was always larger than he and his captains ever knew.

Notes

1. JLCE, 4: 9.
2. Jefferson to Lewis, Washington, D.C., June 20, 1803, in Jackson, ed., *Letters*, 1: 61.
3. Jackson, ed., *Letters*, 1: v.
4. Levi Lincoln to Jefferson, Washington, D.C., April 17, 1803, Jackson, ed., *Letters*, 1: 35.
5. Brian Vickers, ed., *Francis Bacon* (New York: Oxford University Press, 1996), 36.
6. JLCE, 4: 10.
7. Ibid., 4: 226.
8. Lt. James King to Banks, October 1780, in David Mackay, "A Presiding Genius of Exploration: Banks, Cook, and Empire, 1767–1805," in Robin Fisher and Hugh Johnston, eds., *Captain James Cook and His Times* (Seattle: University of Washington Press, 1979), 29.
9. Joseph J. Ellis, *American Sphinx: The Character of Thomas Jefferson* (New York: Alfred A. Knopf, 1997), 193.
10. Jefferson to John Adams, Monticello, June 10, 1815, in Lester J. Cappon, ed., *The Adams-Jefferson Letters*, 2 vols. (Chapel Hill: University of North Carolina Press, 1959), 2: 443.
11. Clark to William Croghan, Fort Mandan, April 2, 1805, Jackson, ed., *Letters*, 1: 230.

THREE

The "Core" of Discovery

We call it the Lewis and Clark expedition. But neither Thomas Jefferson nor his captains used that phrase. For Jefferson it was always "Mr. Lewis's Tour" or the "tour of Lewis and Clark." But sometimes the president called this infantry company on the move "The Corps of Discovery." In recent years that phrase—"The Corps of Discovery"—has become increasingly popular. Like so many of Jefferson's lines, it has a nice ring to it. It sounds good; it sounds right. "Corps of Discovery" appeals to us the same way we like "when in the course of human events" or "life, liberty, and the pursuit of happiness."

These are such wonderful words—so smooth, so engaging, so deceptively familiar. What do they mean? What did the Corps of Discovery "discover" that was not already known to generations of native people? What were Jefferson's explorers commanded to discover? And was the president pleased with what was discovered, uncovered, or even recovered? After all, he confidently told Congress in December 1806 that the Corps of Discovery "had all the success which could have been expected."[1] And just what had Jefferson expected? The simple answer is that more than anything else he expected the discovery of a water passage from Atlantic to Pacific by way of the great rivers Missouri and Columbia. The most important line in Jefferson's instructions to Lewis was the one telling him to locate and explore "the most direct and practicable water communication across this continent for the purposes of commerce."[2] Everything else—all the botany, ethnology, diplomacy, and zoology—was just secondary. As the president once harshly reminded Lewis, "the object of your mission is single, the direct water communication from sea to sea."[3]

But we know, as Lewis and Clark came to know, that Jefferson's dream of a northwest passage was just that—a dream, an illusion, a geographic hat trick; now you see it, now you don't. In the years after 1806 Jefferson struggled to distance himself from that failed dream, talking more about discoveries in the realm of science. Having lost a dream, he set about the more routine business of list making—lists of exotic plants, unusual animals, and mysterious tribal names. Now all of this leaves us with a great puzzle. We like the phrase "Corps of Discovery" but we are stuck with the task of sorting out just what Lewis and Clark really discovered. And our assignment is made all the harder when we acknowledge that theirs were not the first human eyes to see, to discover, to describe, and even to appreciate the country between the Missouri and the Western Sea. But we are fond of the "Corps of Discovery," and liking it means we should think through the meanings of those words.

Possible meanings abound but it seems to me that there are three trails we might follow. But we should know that these trails will not take us to the same destination. Choices made here will determine how we understand the expedition, its journey, and its complex legacies.

FIRST: Like Jefferson we could make lists—lists of plants, animals, cultures, places, and languages new to European and American eyes and ears. But lists are not explanations; they appeal only to cold Reason, and we want something that speaks to both head and heart, mind and soul.

SECOND: We could follow the lead of some recent film makers and popular writers. We could just claim that Lewis and Clark were great discoverers and stay mum about the details. Lewis and Clark are worth your time and attention because I say so—case closed. But of course the meanings are in the details, and assertion is not demonstration.

THIRD: We could try once again to think through just what Jefferson and his Corps of Discovery expected to find (and then did find) beyond the wide Missouri.

This is the choice I would have us make. Jefferson read his books, studied his maps, dreamed his dreams, and then imagined a West. What was the size, the shape, the substance of that lovingly imagined place? As he looked from Monticello west beyond the Blue Ridge, what sort of country came to life in his mind's eye?

It seems to me that in Jefferson's West—that country of the mind out past St. Louis—there were four grand expectations. These were the four cardinal points on his compass; they were his articles of faith about the West. And like all true believers, Jefferson was convinced that reality would assume the shape of his beliefs.

The First Expectation: The Empty West

It has become a cultural, geographic commonplace to call the West "the big empty." That is what writer Gertrude Stein was getting at when she said that the West is more space where nobody is than were anybody is. Tourist brochures, travel agents, and state tourism officials talk about the West as "the wide open spaces" where everything is "high, wide, and lonesome" and everywhere is "miles from nowhere." Of course these are East Coast clichés born out of geographic ignorance, cultural arrogance, and distorted senses of time and distance. But Jefferson believed them, or at least something like them. No matter how much he and his explorers thought about the West, no matter how much attention they paid to native cultures or plants or animals or geography, the country bounded by the Missouri and the Pacific still seemed an empty place. Nothing brings that home with greater force than looking at maps of the West drafted at the time of the expedition. Samuel Lewis's 1803 map of Louisiana is a classic depiction of the empty West. Like a blank slate, the West seemed to invite Americans to write all sorts of messages—personal and national—on its unmarked face. And many westbound Americans did just that in later years, leaving their names carved on places like Independence Rock along the Oregon Trail in present-day Wyoming. The expectation of the empty West seemed not so much a frightening prospect as an inviting promise. It was a promise that said: this is a place made of clay—mold it and shape it whatever way you choose. There are no limits. Here you can make your own Eden, your own paradise. Americans have long responded to the lure of emptiness, filling up places with dreams of their own making and in the process driving out those who had come before.

The Second Expectation: The Wilderness West

It was not just an empty West that Jefferson invented and Lewis and Clark expected to find. They also believed they would find a wilderness West. There are few words in modern American English more slippery, more elusive, more changeable in meaning and use than the word "wilderness." We have used it in negative ways to mean wild, untamed, untouched places, trackless places, territories of risk and danger. Wilderness is the enemy of Civilization. In the wilderness—what New England Puritans called "the howling wilderness"—evil could overwhelm good, doubt could defeat faith.

Wilderness was something to defeat, tame, and domesticate. At the same time, and especially in our century, we have put a positive construction on the word. Now "wilderness" means natural beauty, high adventure, something to embrace and preserve. The very place where the Puritans thought they would lose their souls are now where we think we might find ours.

But such romantic excesses had little or no appeal for Jefferson and his Corps of Discovery. When they envisioned the West as wilderness they conjured up a place where Nature had slipped the chains of Rule and Reason and now ran loose and unchecked. Such a wild place could have no real homes, no genuine families, no enduring civilizations until the wild-ness was beaten down, beaten back, and made to accept the ruling hand of man the farmer, man the honest republican cultivator of the good earth.

The Third Expectation: The Bounded West

The West was, so Jefferson thought, an empty place, a wild place, and also—strangely enough—a place with remarkably clear lines and boundaries. Whether you looked from Mexico City or Washington or Quebec, the country west of the Missouri seemed to be divided up into neat sections, tidy imperial packages. Depending on the nationality of the cartographer and the aspirations of his audience, those packages were either grand in sweep or tightly confined to narrow, coastal parcels. Imagine maps of the Louisiana Purchase drafted by American, Spanish, Canadian, and Mandan cartographers. For an American audience a Purchase map might run along lines from the mouth of the Mississippi to the source of the Missouri—surely the heart of a vast American empire. But a Spanish map would reveal a very different, and much smaller, package. Spanish diplomats, bureaucrats, soldiers, and cartographers all believed that the purchase was no more than present-day Missouri and part of Arkansas. Now that is a very sharply defined, closely confined American West! And the Canadians—who after all had the real jump on the Americans in the Northwest thanks to James Cook, George Vancouver, Peter Pond, and Alexander Mackenzie—how did they carve up the West and hand out the slices? Aaron Arrowsmith's map of 1795 tells the story. In the new British Empire in America after the colonial rebellion of 1776, the West and the Pacific Northwest were the jewels in the crown. From present-day Montana and Idaho to Oregon and Washington by way of British Columbia, the entire West will be—so this London map claims—under royal sway.

For Mandan map-makers—and Lewis and Clark met at least one of them—the very idea of either Louisiana or a purchase made little sense. Why name a country after a distant and now-dead French king? Selling the country was dangerous nonsense, and besides, no plains people had been party to the transaction. But Mandan cartographers did have a sure sense of their own country and the territorial boundaries of the Mandan world. For now at least, the Louisiana Purchase had no place—no real presence— on Indian maps. That, of course, was soon to change.

Such were the clear visions of empire—visions that took no notice of rivals, competitors, or first-comers. And of course, these were the clarities that seduce and ultimately disillusion. So it was with Thomas Jefferson. The West seduced him, promising a place free from racial violence and partisan conflict. It was not until the Missouri Crisis of 1819–21, with its threats of division over slavery, that Jefferson began his road to disillusionment.

The Fourth Expectation: The Simple West

What this first American reconnaissance of the West expected was emptiness, wilderness, clarity, and finally, simplicity. The simple West was at the heart of Jefferson's own mental and political geography. What he took on faith was the following geographic catechism:

1. That the mountains of the West were like those of the East, all arranged in neat parallel ridges and pierced by many passes;
2. That three great rivers of North America—the Ohio, the Missouri, and the Columbia—provided the channels for a trans-continental water highway;
3. And that the interior of North America was a fertile garden, a farmer's paradise with rich soil, abundant water, and a temperate climate. Meriwether Lewis took that image up the Missouri and reported he found "one of the fairest portions of the globe."[4] Here in the garden of the West Americans could be forever free, self-reliant, and in love with liberty. In this garden Americans would flourish safe from the temptations of urban vice and industrial decay.

This was a simple, but not a simple-minded, geography. It was an expression of Jefferson's belief that the West could provide constant renewal and fresh life for the American republic. In the clean balance of mountains, rivers, and gardens, Jefferson found reassurance—reassurance that the victories of the American Revolution would not be lost. This simple West was his insurance policy against an uncertain future.

Empty, wild, clear, simple—these words best describe what Jefferson, Lewis, and Clark believed, hoped, and trusted they would find beyond the wide Missouri and over the Stony Mountains. We find what we look for; we uncover what we seek after. Despite not finding a usable water passage from Atlantic to Pacific, the Corps of Discovery did find much that they had gone in search of. But on every journey, no matter how well planned, there are revelations—uncoveries if you will—that are unlooked for and perhaps even unwelcome.

We can appreciate those surprising discoveries by some sleight-of-hand magic spelling. Instead of talking about the Corps of Discovery and spelling it c-o-r-p-s, we might spell it c-o-r-e, and then ask: what was the core of discovery? What did these travelers learn, even if the learning was done reluctantly and in some confusion? What did they discover about their own cherished beliefs, even if such discoveries tarnished and dented those beliefs? What I'd like to suggest is that the core, the fundamentals proved to be exactly the opposite of what Jefferson and his captains expected.

The explorers expected emptiness and found fullness. They found not the Big Empty but the Big Full. The West of Lewis and Clark, the West of native people like Black Cat, Cameahwait, and Coboway was a place unimaginably full. Here were landscapes filled with plants and animals, sounds and languages, shapes and colors. If there is such a thing as an empty West, it is today with fewer plants, fewer animals, and perhaps less in the diversity of peoples and cultures. We have a little-used word in English to describe the kind of fullness that Lewis and Clark encountered. That word is plenitude, from the Latin *plenus*, meaning complete or full. The West was not a perfect land of plenty, a Native American garden of Eden. Native peoples from the Great Plains to the Pacific Northwest knew all about scarcity and hunger, violence and death. But they did live in a world fuller, more diverse, more richly variegated than we often imagine. Jefferson and his adventurers went into the West expecting empty space. Instead they found countries where the buffalo were so dense that the travelers had to beat a path through the herds. That is an image of fullness, of plenitude that should endure in our national imagination.

The explorers expected wilderness and found home. Nothing puts in sharper focus the different ways Euro-Americans and Native Americans saw the West than to consider two words—"wilderness" and "home." Stand at Fort Clatsop's main gate and ponder those words. In the minds and through the eyes of William Clark and his companions, home was East, someplace else, perhaps Virginia or Kentucky. Wilderness was everything else, every-where else. Clark walked through the gate and into what he imagined a wilderness. How different it was for Coboway and the Clatsops from Point Adams village. All that Clark called wilderness was for them home, back-yard, and neighborhood. What needed exploring for the Clatsops was that odd, rectangular space the bearded strangers called their fort. Lewis and Clark had come upon but never fully understood a core truth about the West. What outsiders called wilderness was in fact home. Who would occupy that home and enjoy its plenitude soon became the heart of what we might call the War for the West. It was a war that began for the United States with Lewis and Clark and in one way or another continues in our own time.

The explorers expected clarity, the clear, well-defined lines of imperial ambition etched on maps from London, Madrid, Philadelphia, or Wash-ington. What Lewis and Clark found was a West far murkier, far more com-plex than they had ever suspected. Without using the word, the explorers had come upon ambiguity. Like all travelers, Lewis and Clark learned that places and events have many sides and many explanations. Individuals have many faces. Things are often not what they seem to be. And in the glare of a plains sun or the shroud of a North Coast fog, the lines of imperial ambition blurred. Grounded in the Enlightenment tradition that cele-brated fact and precision, Lewis and Clark found ambiguity an unwelcome discovery.

The explorers expected simplicity, the simple geography that nourished Jefferson's dream of an empire for liberty. Schooled in the mountains and rivers of the East, Lewis and Clark anticipated finding western terrain that mirrored the familiar lay of the land. But here too they encountered inescapable realities, the facts of land and life in the American West. The geography out past St. Louis did not conform to the simplicities of Enlightenment theory. East to West there was no neat balance of rivers, mountains, passes, and gardens. What the West offered instead was a com-plex tangle of mountain range upon range all interlaced with wild, impass-able rivers. And while some of the West had soil as fertile as any in Ohio or Illinois, other places were never meant for the plow. Out across the Missouri Lewis and Clark did not find a mirror reflecting the East; instead they—like Alice—stepped through the looking-glass and into a world filled with box canyons, twisted trails, and mountains all topsy-turvy.

Realities rarely match expectations. Whether the trip is to the grocery store or some distant planet, what we find is never quite what we thought would be on the shelf. A drive to Paris, Texas is not like an ocean voyage to

Paris, France. Planning the journey, experiencing the journey, and measuring the consequences of the journey—whether to one Paris or the other—is sure to mean riding horses of different colors. And so it was with Jefferson and his Corps of Discovery. The expedition was an enterprise remarkably confident about its goals and the ultimate consequences of reaching those goals. Lewis and Clark never thought about the West as "The Great Unknown." They were fully prepared to encounter the empty, the wild, the simple, and the clearly marked. But what they found is the core of discovery. They found fullness, home, a disturbing ambiguity, and a bewilderingly complex geography. And it is exactly here that Jefferson and Cameahwait, Clark and Coboway, Lewis and Black Cat become our contemporaries. It is just here that the years collapse and the centuries fade away. Like them, we live not in an empty space but in a very full place. Diversity is not an abstraction in American life. It is our reality. Lewis and Clark glimpsed the American crazy quilt; we live in it. And what about where we live? Lewis and Clark expected wilderness and found the homes of native people. Now that all of us have homes on the range, little houses on the prairie, what kind of stewards have we been? How have we cared for America now that it has become, in the words of Wright Morris, "the home place." Neither Jefferson nor his captains appreciated the subtle nuances of ambiguity. They wanted a world with clear choices and well-marked boundaries. And so do we. But modern life is not like that, and Lewis and Clark had an uneasy inkling of the future—a future where moral compasses go spinning and exceptions out-weigh the rules. None of this is simple, and of course simplicity is what the President and his men wanted. They sought a simple geography, a simple future, and a simple American empire with no rivals. What they found is what we live in and through each day. They found complexity. They did not find a Native American paradise or Jefferson's republic of happy farmers or even Henry David Thoreau's forest of true knowledge. Up the Missouri, across the mountains, and down the Columbia the travelers met daily lessons about life in a complex world. Like those adventurers, we struggle to make our way along crooked paths and over broken ground.

At the core of the Lewis and Clark journey are four enduring revelations, revelations that come clear only if we pause to reflect on them.

First, that the natural world was meant to be plenitude, fullness, diversity—not one way but many ways; not one voice and one face but many voices and many faces.

Second, that so much of the history of the West was (and still is) a struggle about home—whose home will it be? And if outsiders come to claim home, do the first-comers, the insiders, the first housekeepers, become strangers, exiles from the promised land. And how long do you have to live here to call it home?

Third, that the lives of individual human beings and great nations can never be told as simple stories with easy plots and comforting conclusions. Lewis and Clark were forced to confront ambiguity, the hard fact that real life is more hazy gray than stark black and white.

Fourth, that everything is more complex than it seems and that real maturity requires accepting complexity—whether that complexity is in geography or human relations.

The novelist Italo Calvino once wrote that "a classic is a book that has never finished saying what it has to say."[5] The Lewis and Clark journey is that sort of book. Reading it, walking along with it, we are rewarded with the promise of enlargement, and the adventure of strangeness. Embracing the core of discovery enlarges our vision, expands our horizons, and serves as a steady reminder that life in the West was and is an unpredictable mix of hope and expectation, despair and disillusion. At the core of discovery is the recognition that all human kind are but travelers making rough journeys, sustained now and again by the kindness of strangers.

Notes

1. Jefferson, Annual Message to Congress, December 2, 1806, Jackson, ed., *Letters*, 1: 352.
2. Jefferson to Lewis, Washington, D.C., June 20, 1803, Jackson, ed., *Letters*, 1: 61.
3. Jefferson to Lewis, Washington, D.C., November 16, 1803, Jackson, ed., *Letters*, 1: 137.
4. Lewis to Lucy Marks, Fort Mandan, March 31, 1805, Jackson, ed., *Letters*, 1: 223.
5. Italo Calvino, "Why Read the Classics?" in Steven Gilbar, ed., *Reading in Bed: Personal Essays on the Glories of Reading* (Boston: David R. Godine, 1995), 91.

Map Portfolio
Maps and Storied Landscapes

In early March 1803, as Congress prepared to adjourn and Thomas Jefferson looked forward to a summer at Monticello, French ambassador Louis André Pichon paid one last call on the third president of the United States. If the ambassador thought the visit was simple diplomatic courtesy, he soon learned otherwise. Pichon found himself the only student in an impromptu lecture on western geography and exploration. Turning to a large 1802 Arrowsmith map of North America, Jefferson traced what became the Lewis and Clark route up the Missouri, across the Rockies, and down the Columbia to the sea. As Pichon later reported, the president "explained his purpose to me" by means of the map. In retrospect this seems a simple historical moment. Jefferson the imperial storyteller told part of the Lewis and Clark story to a European diplomat. The map was the president's silent partner, present only to illustrate what the narrator had to say.

But the Arrowsmith map and all its cartographic cousins were considerably more than mute witnesses in the exploration drama. Like the explorers who made and used them, maps were storytellers. And they remain so today. They speak to us in the voices of desire and imagination, hope and expectation. Just as much as words, maps called landscapes into being. We sometimes view maps as reflections of terrain in the physical world. But maps do more than mirror the world; they create and compose it. They reveal what John Allen calls "patterns of promise." What did the maps printed here promise those who drew them and those who shaped their lives by what they revealed?

The promises were many, and what they offered recalls some of the earliest and most compelling European dreams about the New World. Looking now at the maps crafted by Peter Pond, Jedediah Morse, and Samuel Lewis we are stuck by the presence of emptiness. And that emptiness carried a powerful message for audiences who looked to such maps for knowledge about the West, and perhaps the very meaning of the West as well. By their seeming emptiness these maps of the West promised new beginnings. They envisioned the West as a blank slate on which to inscribe American texts of independence, self-reliance, and prosperity. Those same maps promised a geography of rivers and mountains that made what historical geographer D. W. Meinig calls "the outward movement" seem an act determined and blessed by Nature. River highways, gentle mountains, and a western ocean close at hand all appeared as Nature's signs of a bright future. And there was a political-imperial promise as well. The maps in this portfolio advanced a vision of an American empire unchallenged by the presence of native people or the designs of European rivals. In the struggle for the West, such maps promised bloodless invasion, peaceful conquest, and untroubled possession.

These promises were wrapped around two compelling national narratives, each a key part of an emerging American identity. In the first story, an American Adam and Eve could find a home in the Garden of the World, their journey made easy by an all-wise, all-beneficent Nature. Once there this American family would take root and flourish in a fertile country safe from the vices of the corrupt and corrupting East. Reversing the biblical sequence, these maps told a story of Americans making their exodus to the West and then finding a genesis in the New World garden. Americans could duplicate Exodus and Genesis with the promise that the western garden had no temptations and no fall from republican grace. That story, inspired by the seventeenth-century Puritan migrations and firmly embedded in the American cultural vocabulary, was joined by one from the Enlightenment. Here the narrative was all about journeys in search of knowledge to build empires both intellectual and territorial. Exploration patrons saw maps like the ones printed here as proof of the steady progress of the Known and the inevitable shrinking of the Unknown. Jefferson could have been thinking about these maps and their landscapes when he told William Dunbar that future generations of explorers would "fill up the canvas we begin." Promises and stories—these maps spring from all the passions and desires that shaped exploration journeys into the West.

What Wallace Stegner once called "the geography of hope" is written all over these maps. Every river is navigable, no mountain stands as a barrier to a westering people, and the country beyond St. Louis is bound to be William Blake's "green and pleasant land." But two centuries after these maps were drafted, the countries of promise they so eagerly portrayed seem more what the English novelist D. H. Lawrence called "the coasts of illusion." The Platte and the Yellowstone were not western versions of the Ohio and the Hudson. The Rockies posed challenges unimagined by those who once crossed the Appalachians. And the soils of the Great Plains could not sustain the farming ways of the Old Northwest. But no matter the realities; the illusions often seemed more compelling than the hard faces of western facts. Explorers shaped their journeys and their maps to the outlines of those illusions. Dreams die hard and fantasy often seems to have a life of its own. Even so skilled a cartographer as William Clark was not immune from the seductive illusion of the water passage. A close look at the great map that accompanied publication of Nicholas Biddle's *History of the Expedition under the Command of Captains Lewis and Clark* in 1814 reveals a ghost river called the Multnomah rising near the headwaters of the Yellowstone, Arkansas, Platte, and other western rivers. The Multnomah was Clark's misreading of the present-day Willamette River. That misreading was based on desire and a persistent faith in the presence of the passage. If the Missouri and Columbia connection was not the passage, then perhaps the Multnomah was the link between eastern waters and the Columbia. John Allen calls the Multnomah "the river of necessity." It was there because it had to be present in the landscape.

These maps remind us that the geographic exploration of the West never moved in a straight line, progressing from simple illusion to complex reality. Geographic knowledge was (and remains) an accumulation of old images and new bits of information—all filtered through and molded by imagination. Maps sometimes have a cool look about them as if declaring that they are Reason's children. But we should consider maps as the creative expressions of passion, ambition, and desire. As the essayist Umberto Eco reminds us, the "force of the false" is always more powerful than we imagine. Explorers and cartographers drew their maps and made their journeys guided by the twin stars of Hope and Illusion. Neither western star would soon lose its power to attract and deceive.

Collection of the author

1. Peter Pond, Map of the Northwest, 1790.

First published in *Gentleman's Magazine*, March 1790, Pond's map of the Northwest tells a powerful story about possible routes to the Pacific Ocean. As the most influential fur-trade geographer and strategist of the age, Pond drew on first-hand experience, information collected from Indians, and current geographical lore to create a compelling image of the West. Reflecting the geographic wisdom of the time, Pond sketched the Rocky Mountains as a single, narrow range relatively close to the Pacific Ocean. Pond's Northwest Passage was a river connection between the Great Slave Lake and the Pacific Ocean by way of the ghost waterway, Cook's River. Pond's map was both an image of the West and a strategy for building a western empire. His ideas had a profound influence on Alexander Mackenzie and Thomas Jefferson.

44

2. Antoine Pierre Soulard, Map of Western North America, 1795 (French version).

Drafted in St. Louis by Surveyor-General Antoine Pierre Soulard at the request of Spanish officials, this map reflects years of trader experience up the Missouri as well as preparation for the important Mackay-Evans expedition of 1795–97. Soulard also incorporated geographic lore about the Northwest Passage, showing the Missouri River trending toward the Pacific. In the English version of the map carried by Lewis and Clark, the Oregan or River of the West heads from the Pacific toward the Rockies to almost join with the Missouri.

46

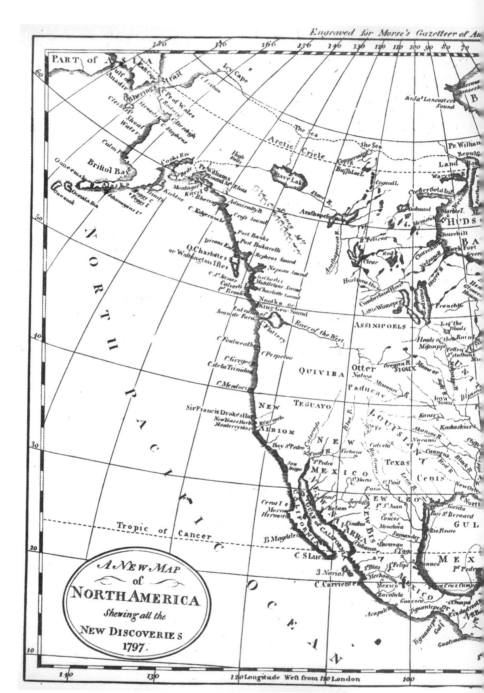

Collection of John L. Allen

**3. Jedediah Morse,
"A New Map of North
America Shewing
All the New Discoveries
1797," published in Morse's
*New American Universal
Geography,* 1801.**

No geographer was more
widely known in the early
republic than Jedediah
Morse. His books and
maps educated at least two
generations of Americans
about the continent and its
imperial future. This map
contains many layers of
western geographic lore
including the continued
presence of Quivira, the
River of the West, and
Peter Pond's dream of
Cook's River flowing from
the Great Slave Lake to the
Pacific. And in all of this
Morse managed to erase
the Rockies.

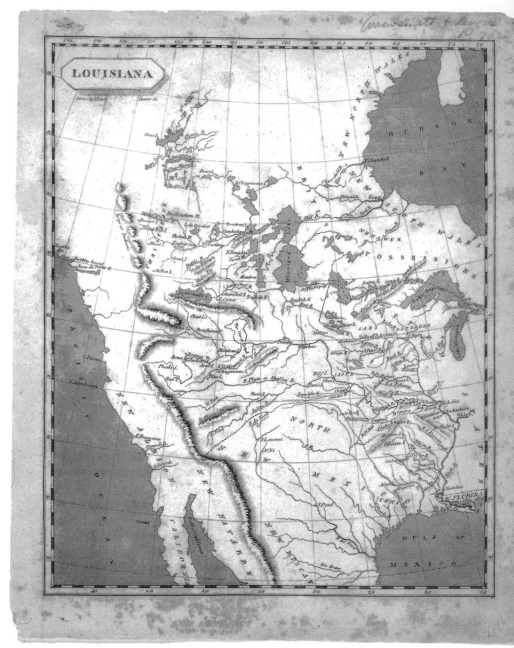

Collection of the author

4. Samuel Lewis, "Louisiana," 1804.

Prepared for inclusion in Aaron Arrowsmith's *A New and Elegant General Atlas of North America*, no single printed map of the period more fully embodied how Jefferson and his contemporaries envisioned the West. River systems promise a quick passage across the continent and the single ridge of the Rockies is no barrier to that passage. The West itself appears as a well-watered space ready to be settled and farmed by stalwart republicans.

Courtesy of the Library of Congress

**5. Nicholas King, Map of
the American West, 1803.**

One of the maps carried by
Lewis and Clark and based
on the best available information current in 1803, this
map represents what John L.
Allen describes as "probably
the most precise American
image of the western interior
before Lewis and Clark."
The map portrays the
Missouri River heading
toward the Rockies and hints
at the Columbia reaching
out to meet that stream.
But all of this is labeled as
"conjectural." King made no
effort at depicting western
mountains, focusing instead
on the river system that
Jefferson hoped Lewis and
Clark would find.

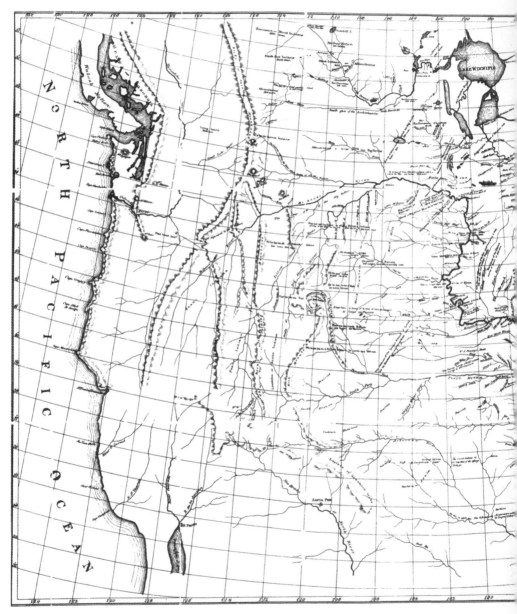

Collection of John L. Allen

6. William Clark, "A Map of part of the Continent of North America," 1805. Copied by Nicholas King.

Prepared during the winter at Fort Mandan (1804–5), this map represents Clark's effort to understand the West and predict the expedition's route into it based on geographic lore, travel experience thus far, and information gathered from Indian sources. At this point Clark's West was still Jefferson's dream country, a place where Americans could make the national mark on an unmarked landscape. Clark remained confident that a river passage did exist across the continent and that the Rockies would be no barrier to that journey.

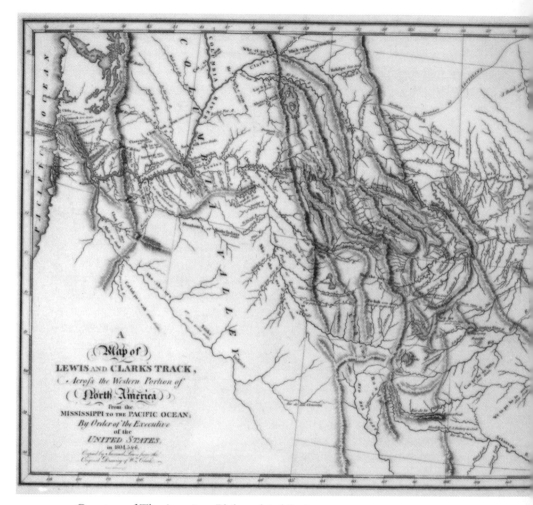

A

(Map of)

LEWIS AND CLARKS TRACK,

Across the Western Portion of

((North America))

From the

MISSISSIPPI to the PACIFIC OCEAN,

By Order of the Executive

of the

UNITED STATES,

in 1804 5 & 6.

Courtesy of The American Philosophical Society

7. William Clark, "A Map of Lewis and Clark's Track," published in Nicholas Biddle, *History of the Expedition under the Command of Captains Lewis and Clark,* 1814. Engraved by Samuel Lewis from Clark's 1810 master map.

Perhaps no map in this sequence tells more influential stories than this one. The landmark cartographic contribution of the Lewis and Clark expedition, the 1814 Track Map held on to old illusions while proclaiming new truths. The ghost river Multnomah kept the simple passage dream alive. At the same time Clark presented a

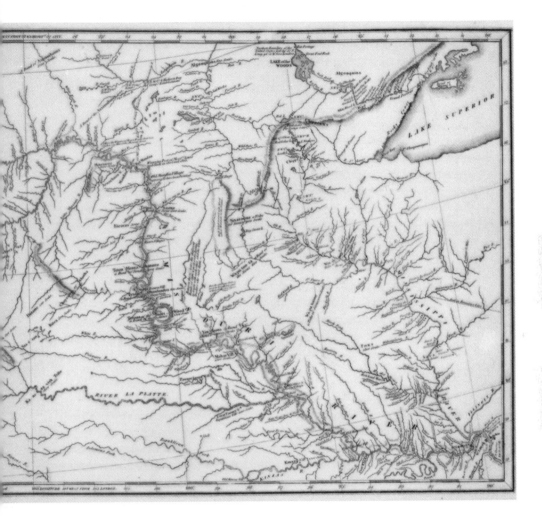

West far more topographically diverse than Jefferson ever imagined. Clark now knew that the Rockies were a tangle of mountain ridges and that western rivers were not the navigable waterways proposed in Jefferson's geography of hope. Despite what future generations of promoters and developers might promise, this map made it clear that the West was not an undifferentiated garden, not just another Ohio or Illinois beyond the Missouri. The recognition of western regionalism began with this map. As an act of political imagination the map advanced an American imperial agenda—one that acknowledged an Indian presence while ignoring Spanish and British claims in the West. In the largest sense the 1814 map is Manifest Destiny visualized.

FOUR

Imagining the West
Through the Eyes of Lewis and Clark

The best history focuses not so much on an idea as on a question. As David Hackett Fischer writes, "questions are the engines of intellect."[1] We learn most things in our lives by asking questions—how does it work, where does it come from, what does it mean, what should I do next? The Lewis and Clark story has often been told with declarative sentences, moving the explorers' narrative from one place to another at a seemingly inevitable pace. But Thomas Jefferson knew that exploration was powered by questions. It was a set of questions that created the first American expedition to the Pacific and then guided it on what William Clark called its "road across the continent."[2] So let me pose a question prompted by some twenty years of reading the Lewis and Clark journals, traveling the expedition's trail, and thinking about the exploration of the early North American West. Let me warn you in advance. This is a deceptive question. It may sound easy to answer but the search will probably take us in unexpected directions. And my guess is that the answers offered will be a bit unsettling. But then all discovery and exploration is unsettling and perhaps even troubling.

With that as caution, the question is: What did the West look like to Lewis and Clark? Did the members of the Corps of Discovery come to realize that there was not one West but many Wests? How did those Wests appear to eyes and minds so comfortable with familiar eastern landscapes? What does it mean when we read Sgt. John Ordway describing what is now Fergus county, Montana as "the desert of North America," a place wholly unfit for any human life?[3] And Sgt. Patrick Gass agreed, calling that part of the Treasure State "the most dismal country I ever beheld."[4] Lewis and Clark journal keepers said equally unflattering things about the present states of

Idaho, Washington, and Oregon. Such words seem strangely out of place to our modern sensibility. It is as if Ordway and Gass were seeing another world, one now lost to us. Do such landscape vocabularies mean that Thomas Jefferson's Corps of Discovery could never escape its eastern past? Let me ask the question again. What did the Corps of Discovery see in the West? Seeing is not just a physiological act. The old rule from first-year physics applies here: to every observation the observer brings something. The expedition saw the whole western landscape through eastern eyes. The *East* was not simply an abstraction for these travelers. The East was home. It offered a different sense of space and distance, a place where the horizon was sometimes made invisible by a canopy of trees. The East was rolling country made green by seasonable rain. The East meant navigable rivers, mountains with passes and water gaps, and above all a landscape made familiar by entire lifetimes of experience. But those eyes were not blind to new shapes and colors, unexpected weather, and unanticipated distances. Like us, they saw in a glass darkly. If we understand that seeing means more than just looking, then we can begin to re-imagine the West through explorers' eyes.

Many of us would have a simple, quick way to answer the question about the West that Lewis and Clark encountered. We would march off to our favorite museum or perhaps page through a lavish book of western art until we came to the magnificent paintings and drawings of George Catlin, Karl Bodmer, and Paul Kane. There, in those artistic visions, were the landscapes of the West just as Lewis and Clark saw them. Question answered, case closed. But as Sherlock Holmes and Sam Spade knew, no case is ever really closed, no question is ever fully answered. We might think of exploration as "seeing" and our understanding of it in this way. Lewis and Clark laid one main line of exploration track from east to west. That main line was important, but it showed them only one piece of a vast and vastly complex country. Three decades later when Catlin and Bodmer rode the Lewis and Clark Missouri River trunk line they took it only into Montana. It is important for us to remember that while Lewis and Clark saw only one slice of the western pie, the pioneer documentary artists painted an even thinner slice of that pie. Not only was the Catlin and Bodmer geographic range a sharply limited one but it was also an artistic vision interested only in a few things. Catlin's bright colors and Bodmer's wonderful eye for detail can trick us into a romantic, technicolor West. So we are back to the original question—What did the West look like to Lewis and Clark? How can we recapture what they saw without denying that landscape meanings and cultural vocabularies have changed profoundly over two centuries?

I think there is a way for us to do that. I've always thought that the eye of the mind and the power of print are the real secrets to recovering a sense of the past. The force of the imagination carried Thomas Jefferson into the West, transporting him far beyond the Blue Ridge Mountains. That same force was present in the lives of travelers as different as Meriwether Lewis, John Ordway, and Patrick Gass. We need to read thoughtfully and listen carefully to the words of the explorers themselves. Simple, memorable words from explorers' journals can give wings to our imaginations and take us back to another time.

Before there were visual images of the West for European and American audiences there were words—words describing the West as both geography and state of mind. Those words—and the powerful, seductive ideas expressed by them, and in them, and through them—came from the imaginations and experiences of entrepreneurs, adventurers, promoters, and explorers. What they wrote gave shape and substance to a West both imagined and real. Explorers and their patrons invented the West, or rather, they invented the meanings of the West. What William Goetzmann has memorably called the "West of the Imagination" was a wonderland of the fantastic and the marvelous. Here the exotic was commonplace and the erotic seemed to beckon with eager embrace. The words fashioned a timeless place where the dead hand of the past held no sway, where life could begin afresh at the dawn of creation. This West dressed in brighter colors, breathed purer air, and danced along virtue's path. Whether the dreams were of fur or gold, land or oil, the West seemed Eden come back to earth. Nature itself seemed larger and more immediate. Elemental forces here fought on a vast scale to create signs in rock and water—signs of wonder, awe, and majesty.

This West had to be verbalized before it could be visualized. The tangled chaos of prairies, mountains, deserts, and forests had to be reduced to words and text. Writing about what they saw or thought they saw, explorers composed the country and made it a landscape. As Willa Cather wrote in *My Ántonia*, the West was "nothing but land: not a country at all, but the material out of which countries are made."[5] In letters, journals, and formal reports explorers gave readers a set of expectations, prefabricated experiences about the West. Explorers set the context, defined the limits before any artist put brush to canvas. The colors of the mental palette were mixed in a swirl of explorers' words and texts. Artists saw the West first not as image but as word. To appreciate the images we must begin with the words.

Some of the earliest and most powerful words in English about the West came from the journal keepers of the Lewis and Clark Expedition. While John Charles Frémont was more widely read in the nineteenth century, it was Lewis and Clark who set the aesthetic pattern—a pattern that William

Clark put simply when he surveyed the landscape around the Great Falls of the Missouri and wrote, "this country has a romantic appearance."[6] Explorers like Lewis and Clark did more than describe landscapes. They composed scenes, arranging words to express visual images that fit contemporary ideas about the sublime and the beautiful. In early July 1804, the Lewis and Clark expedition was making its way up the Missouri on the border between present-day Kansas and Nebraska. After camping near the mouth of the Big Nemaha (in what is now Holt County, Missouri), Clark led a small party some three miles up that stream to survey the countryside. Climbing an Indian mound above the river, Clark paused to look at a world of flowing water, trees of many kinds, and a sea of tall grass. Later that day, when it was time to put nature into words, Clark took those raw materials and made a landscape. As Simon Schama writes in *Landscape and Memory*, "landscapes are culture before they are nature; constructs of the imagination projected onto wood and water and rock."[7] What Clark constructed was no ordinary landscape; it followed broad cultural understandings of what was beautiful, balanced, and sublime. The explorer shaped the relationships between trees, water, and grass just as would any eighteenth-century English garden architect. Even the idea of describing the scene from a prospect—an elevated point—was as much an artistic convention as surveyor's common sense.

> From the top of the highest of those Mounds I had an extensive view of the Serounding Plains, which afforded one of the most pleasing prospects I ever beheld, under me a Butifull River of Clear water of about 80 yards Meandering thro: a leavel and extensive Meadow, as far as I could See, the view of the prospect Much enlivened by the fine Trees and Srubs which is bordering the bank of the river, and the Creeks and runs falling into it. The bottom land is covered with Grass of about 4 and a half feet high, and appears as leavel as a Smoth Surface. The second bottom is also covered with Grass and rich weeds and flours, interspersed with Copses of the Osage Plumb. On the rising lands, Small groves of trees are Seen, with a numbers of Grapes and a Wild Cherry resembling the Common Wild Cherry, only larger and grows on a Small bush on the tops of those hills in every direction.[8]

What a geologist might have described as the broad floodplain prairies of the Big Nemaha, Clark re-composed as a romantic landscape. What an archaeologist would have noted as the location of a late prehistoric Oneota village known today as the Leary site, Clark re-made as a green Eden. All that was lacking was the artist's brush, canvas, and paint.

The most important journeys are the ones made before leaving home. They are the travels in the country of the mind. We should begin where the Lewis and Clark expedition began, not in St. Louis, but in the spacious mind of Thomas Jefferson. Like all those explorers who sailed and tracked North America before them, Lewis and Clark were guided by a vision of where they were going and what their journey might mean. Such visions combined expectations about landscapes imagined but not yet seen and hopes for rewards at the end of the voyage. What Lewis and Clark had with them was Jefferson's design, one that he fashioned by blending his own thoughts with what he had read about the memorable voyages of James Cook, George Vancouver, and Alexander Mackenzie. Jefferson's captains believed they were seeing the West through his eyes and by his design. If we want to know what Lewis and Clark saw or imagined they saw, we must begin with the words and vision of the third president of the United States.

Some twenty years before drafting exploration instructions for what became the Lewis and Clark expedition, Thomas Jefferson set down his earliest thoughts about the American West in a landmark book. *Notes on the State of Virginia* was his only published book, and Jefferson made it a compendium of all his reading and thinking about the world he knew best. At first glance, *Notes* seems not much more than Jefferson's report on the state of his home state. But he meant to write beyond Virginia's political borders. For him, Virginia was another way to say America. Virginia's colonial boundaries had once run from ocean to ocean; dreams of a greater Virginia did not quickly fade. To describe Virginia was to define America.

As Jefferson suggested in *Notes*, this Virginia-as-America had a geography that invited territorial expansion westward. Jefferson evaluated rivers by their navigability and the Missouri—the "principal river" of the western country—seemed to promise a passage deep into the interior of the continent. St. Louis traders, so Jefferson heard, had already gone some two thousand miles up the Missouri. Perhaps the Missouri headwaters were close to where other great rivers rose, making a water passage to the Pacific more than a fanciful dream. In a world where nature was all in balance and one edge of the continent mirrored the other, mountains would be no barrier to a Pacific passage. Jefferson reported that eastern mountains were not "scattered confusedly over the face of the country" but arranged in neat, parallel ridges.[9] Western mountains were sure to be the same. Most important, America's mountains were not wall-like barriers sealing the West off from a restless nation. The force of nature had pierced eastern mountains with convenient gaps and passes; surely nature had done the same in the West.

Jefferson's continental geography as expressed in *Notes* made empire not only possible but somehow almost predetermined. It was as if nature had created and then marked a path for Americans heading west. Years later the expansionist-minded Secretary of State John Quincy Adams made that imperial geography even more explicit, declaring that the "finger of nature" pointed the United States to the Pacific.[10] In Jefferson's mind nature itself also seemed to provide incentives for looking west. *Notes* offered its readers an American nature defined by bounty and promise. Knowing that some European scholars, including the influential French naturalist Comte de Buffon, maintained that the New World produced humans, plants, and animals smaller and less vital than those in the Old World, Jefferson devoted long sections in *Notes* to a spirited defense of the American environment. He included long lists of plants, showing the great diversity in American flora. And there were also lists of animals, comparing size and weight of those in America and Europe. All of this was aimed at demonstrating that American nature did not degrade life; it enhanced creation itself. The West was the garden of the world, and some years later Jefferson proclaimed that "the land yields an abundance of all the necessaries of life, and almost spontaneously."[11] Little wonder that Lewis and Clark went up the Missouri and saw Eden.

When it came time to consider those native people who already lived in the western garden, Jefferson was of two minds. What he admired about Indians were those aspects of native life that seemed most like his own idealized vision of Euro-American society. Oratory, honor, courage, and devotion to family were values and habits Jefferson prized and hoped to secure for life in the new republic. If Indians and Americans grew more alike, they could share a common country and a common destiny. In a moment of effusive optimism, Jefferson told one Indian delegation that white Americans had "been so long here that we seem like you to have grown out of this land: we consider ourselves no longer as of the old nations beyond the great water, but as united in one family with our red brethren here."[12] But if native people rejected American ways and the imperial domain of the republic, the future was grim. The West might be a temporary refuge for native people removed from their eastern lands, but if those same Indians and their western relatives resisted eventual American settlement beyond the Missouri then they would be destroyed. As he explained to William Henry Harrison in 1803, Indians on both sides of the Missouri needed to know that "we have only to shut our hand to crush them."[13]

In *Notes on the State of Virginia*, Jefferson fashioned a text that invented an *American* West long before sending Lewis and Clark to find such a place.

Drawing on his own experience as well as his republican ideals, Jefferson conjured up a West quite unlike those imagined by other exploration patrons. His West was not Cibóla or Quivira. The American West had no place for Spanish treasure seekers in search of lost gold mines or Inca empires on the Great Plains. Jefferson's West was not a fur hunter's paradise where beaver pelts lured solitary adventurers beyond civilization and enriched the treasuries of powerful monopoly companies. This was not to be a West where a few wealthy families owned vast estates, keeping land and water for themselves. Jefferson's West—and the hopeful geography that seemed to make it possible—was a fertile landscape shaped by farmsteads, schoolyards, and tidy villages. This was to be a green and pleasant West, one that would sustain generations of sturdy, self-reliant Americans. By the time Jefferson came to write directions for Lewis and Clark, this imaginary West had become a place as real as Monticello or Philadelphia. Because it had to be there, it would be there. All Lewis and Clark needed to do was follow nature's path.

There is no more familiar nor more important document in western American exploration history than the instructions Jefferson drafted for Meriwether Lewis in the early summer of 1803. Every exploring party sent into the West after 1803 marched with those Jeffersonian orders firmly in mind. It was both text and map. We tend to think about that piece of paper as guidelines for the explorers, a kind of shooting script for Jefferson's great western movie. And indeed it was that, but it was something more as well. The instructions give us clues toward deciphering Jefferson's own dreams, expectations, and fears about the future of the West in the American republic. What he thought he would see if he went up the Missouri, across the mountains, and down the Columbia can help us understand what Lewis and Clark encountered on their real journey.

Reading the instructions as a commentary on Jefferson's mind and imagination reveals some fascinating and important things. Like his counterparts in London, Quebec, and Mexico City, Jefferson assumed that the West was already a battlefield, an arena where the great imperial powers would fight it out for the control of the West and the ultimate destiny of all North America. Always able to balance several opposing ideas at the same time, Jefferson imagined the West as both contested terrain and the Garden of the World. But looking West from Monticello in the summer of 1802, there did seem to be more contest in the West than peaceful Eden. After all, the American continent had been both battleground and prize since 1492. And native people had been struggling against each other for the first conquest of America long before 1492. Jefferson was determined to make the United

States an imperial contender. It was Alexander Mackenzie's vision of British dominion in the West, as expressed in the last section of his book *Voyages from Montreal*, that proved the immediate cause for the Lewis and Clark Expedition. Reading Mackenzie's dream of empire moved Jefferson to enter the struggle. What he had done before was mere playing at the imperial game; Mackenzie's words made Jefferson a real imperialist. Like many of the republican contemporaries, Jefferson was reluctant to use the word *empire*. When he did employ it, empire was always in the presence of an acceptable word like liberty. The word *empire* does not appear in Jefferson's instructions to Lewis. Instead, he decided to use another word often connected to imperial and territorial expansion. The word is *commerce*, a word broadly defined as nearly all productive, profit-oriented human activity. Jefferson and other imperial visionaries knew that business enterprise and national empires were always partners in territorial expansion. When the president ordered his captains to find a passage from Atlantic to Pacific "for the purposes of commerce" he put the United States on the list of combatants in the war for America. That struggle would, in one way or another, shape the entire course of American history.

Thomas Jefferson had the mind and sensibilities of a geographer. He thought in geographic terms and wrote knowingly about the landscape world around him. He read geographic texts and studied maps. Most maps of the West available to Jefferson before the expedition portrayed an uncluttered, nearly empty region. While Jefferson did not envision the kind of geographic complexity we know in the West today, he also did not think it was a simple, nearly featureless place. While mountains intrigued him, it was rivers that engaged him, both as a geographer and an imperial planner. Thinking about the Virginia world he knew, the president expected Lewis and Clark to find a western country equally filled with navigable rivers. Their names run though the instructions like a shining thread—the Missouri, the Columbia, the Oregan, the Colorado, and the ghost river Río Bravo.

In a life filled with making words, sending letters, and reading texts, Jefferson always paid special attention to his farm and garden books. In them he reported experiments with new plants, annual crop yields, and the changing seasons. And in that same spirit, Jefferson once told Charles Willson Peale that while he was an old man, "I am but a young gardener."[14] This devoted gardener put new plants and animals high on the Lewis and Clark priority list. Jefferson anticipated that his explorers would find a West overflowing with plants and animals new to European science and useful for future Americans. But it is important to remember that Jefferson expected particular kinds of plants and animals in the West. Science in Jefferson's time was natural history, a way of looking at the physical world that emphasized utility. Knowledge was valued in direct proportion to its practical application. Like his contemporaries, Jefferson was interested in useful knowledge. That meant botany, zoology, and other sciences with immediate practical, economic consequences. Reading those farm and garden books that he kept so carefully is a reminder that Jefferson's garden of the West was going to be planted with vegetables, not flowers. William Bartram, Jefferson's gardening contemporary and a landscape Romantic, might have wanted samples of the gumbo evening primrose or the checker lily. What Jefferson sought for Monticello's garden were new varieties of corn and tobacco.

When it came to matters of the West, Jefferson was as much the Romantic as a man of the Enlightenment. As Joseph J. Ellis writes in *American Sphinx: The Character of Thomas Jefferson*, the Virginian had a "nearly mystical sense of the American West."[15] When Jefferson thought about the West, cool Reason slipped away as passion and enthusiasm colored what he wrote and said. He was surely not alone in this. Generations of explorers and their patrons had eagerly projected their most fantastic dreams on to the screen of an imagined golden West. Spanish adventurers like Francisco Vásquez de Coronado sought Cibóla among the Zuñi pueblos and Quivira in Kansas. Jean Nicollet, coming ashore at what is now Green Bay, Wisconsin, dressed himself in silk robes ready to meet Chinese mandarins. And countless travelers went in search of the ever-elusive Northwest Passage. By the end of the eighteenth century tales of golden cities and a vast, inland Sea of the West seemed less credible. But the notion of the West as a land of wonder and astonishment would not die. Jefferson the geographer considered this fantasy landscape and was persuaded that it might contain salt mountains, volcanoes, and animals now gone from eastern shores. Charles Willson Peale had only recently uncovered a mammoth skeleton in Orange county, New York and put those bones on display in a special room at the American Philosophical Society in Philadelphia. Might not living mammoths still thunder in the West?

But this West of wonder meant more than the strange and the exotic. Jefferson never imagined the West as simply a museum filled with exhibits to entertain American tourists. In his geography of hope the West promised escape and renewal. From a world increasingly urban and commercial, escape seemed essential. Republican virtue and the future of the nation depended on the culture of agriculture. If Americans remained in the East they would be swallowed up by a profit-mad world, one that offered a future of vice and decay. Escape was necessary; the West promised not only refuge but renewal. In the West Americans could outrun the past, wipe the slate clean, and begin again. The West seemed to guarantee that Americans could re-invent themselves, sloughing off the past like a snake its skin. Part of Jefferson's mystical faith in the power of the West was that out beyond the Missouri, in the Garden of the World, old wounds and rankling animosities would be healed and forgotten. The West was Eden before the fall. It was and would always be the Peaceable Kingdom, the Republic of Virtue. From Lewis and Clark to those who journeyed on the Oregon Trail, no dream would be more compelling and perhaps more disappointing than this one.

Jefferson's vision of the West as a wonderland and cultural fountain of youth was his most dangerous fantasy. But his final expectation was anything but illusory. Consider again the president's instructions for Lewis. Nearly half of the document deals with native people, either as objects of scientific study or as important peoples and tribes to be reckoned with. Jefferson understood one of the fundamental western realities—that the region was not an empty space, an unpopulated place. Lewis and Clark had many Indian missions—everything from diplomacy to ethnography. And in all of those duties Jefferson recognized what became the expedition's almost daily experience. The West was Indian country. Throughout the instructions Jefferson acknowledged what only a few maps hinted at—that the West's first explorers had already scouted the land and called it home.

How did Lewis and Clark see the West and then report it to Jefferson and a wider audience? It seems obvious to say that Meriwether Lewis and William Clark saw the West through the eyes and expectations of their commander-in-chief. But seeing, understanding, and explaining are always more complex than that. Lewis and Clark did share some of Jefferson's notions but they also carried with them their own personal experiences and temperaments. Meriwether Lewis saw a natural history West, one filled with plants and animals no European scholar had yet seen or described. Lewis expressed that sense of the abundant West when writing to his mother from Fort Mandan at the end of March 1805. "From previous information," explained the explorer, "I had been led to believe that it [the plains] was barren, steril, and sandy." But what Lewis discovered instead was a landscape "fertile in the extreme."[16] And he also brought along second-hand memories of Indian warfare in the dark and bloody ground of Kentucky and Tennessee. Those recollections came boiling out during the Fort Clatsop winter of 1805–6 when Lewis warned his companions that Indians were savages at heart and could never be trusted. William Clark saw the

West with a cartographer's eye, paying attention to courses and distances, river currents and mountain trails. Clark family history, bound to matters of planting and speculating, made William's maps and surveys an expression of hope for a landed empire of the sort Jefferson dreamed. His past, and the past of his brother George Rogers Clark, had plenty of Indian-white violence in it but Clark somehow managed to keep those memories at bay. It was Clark who courted native people, listened to their stories, and made friends with men like the Mandan chief Black Cat. Jefferson's text gave Lewis and Clark an exploration context, not a set of blinders.

Saying the names Lewis and Clark can mislead us into thinking that the leaders were the same as the entire expedition. Donald Jackson's injunction about the journey as the product of many minds is worth remembering here. Meriwether Lewis and William Clark were not the only members of the Corps of Discovery to see the West and transform experience into written form. Sergeant John Ordway, a literate and perceptive member of the expedition, kept a journal that described a West more homely than imperial. Ordway saw Indian houses, cornfields, weapons, and cooking pots. His was a countryman's West, one far from the Enlightenment salons of London and Paris. Sergeant Patrick Gass, sometime carpenter by trade, saw much the same thing. And another journal keeper, Private Joseph Whitehouse, was drawn to what historical geographers call the vernacular landscape. This was the world of the everyday, the routines that shape all human life. What we have lost are the "seeings" of George Drouillard, the Shawnee-French hunter, the French-Omaha boatman and one-eyed fiddler Pierre Cruzatte, and the Shoshone woman Sacagawea. What members of the expedition saw came to them through the image filters fashioned long before leaving home. Each experience up the Missouri and across the mountains was measured and described in terms of what had happened before setting out. And it was not simply the experiences of daily life before the journey that shaped what the travelers saw. Whether recognizing it or not, each explorer had imagined the journey. Those imaginings were ever-present as the Corps of Discovery threaded its way through the West. Lewis, Clark, Ordway, Gass and all the other travelers saw the present through the eyes of the past. Recognizing all of this, we can begin to consider what the Corps of Discovery "saw" in a far country.

Beginning piano students all know "Five Easy Pieces," a set of musical exercises that stretch fingers and minds. Lewis and Clark had their own five easy pieces. These were the things they saw and the meanings they gave them. Not all the pieces were easy or fit neatly into the pattern that the president had set for his explorers. Some of the pieces were troubling and others confusing. But in each case what members of the expedition saw and put down on paper has become part of the way we see and understand the early American West. Their pieces have become ours; we see through their eyes.

The first piece was an unexpected one. The Corps of Discovery moved through a remarkably urban, thickly settled West. This did not fit their expectations, nor does it match ours. We tend to think that if ever any party of travelers should have seen the wide open spaces it was Lewis and Clark. But their journals and maps tell a very different story. Everywhere they went, the explorers found Indian communities, some thriving and others abandoned in the face of epidemic disease or the threat of violence. At one time or another those communities were large, well-established towns. It is important to recall that in 1804 more people lived out their daily lives in the five Mandan and Hidatsa towns than called St. Louis home. The Indian agricultural towns of the Missouri River were flourishing communities. We need to remember that towns like Mitutanka, Rooptahee, and Menetarra were home to farmers and merchants long before the map held names like Pierre, Mobridge, Bismarck, and Williston. Across the Great Divide and down the Columbia the explorers found the same urban reality. Stick lodges, wickiups, teepees, and great plank houses—here was a land of towns and villages. We might think of the Lewis and Clark expedition as one community moving through the lands and lives of other communities. What the American explorers saw as empty wilderness was in fact someone else's neighborhood and backyard, someone else's homeplace and workplace.

If Lewis and Clark saw a West already dotted with towns and villages, they also saw a region of astounding human diversity. Here perhaps neither Jefferson nor his explorers were quite ready for such variety. Jefferson knew the West was filled with native people but he could not have guessed at the rich cultural complexity of the Great Plains, the Rockies, the Plateau, and the Pacific Northwest. As fortune had it, the expedition passed through four of the most important native American culture areas. During the winter at Fort Mandan the explorers saw the world of the village farmers, those earth lodge people who made the Dakota soil bloom long before the days of dams, John Deere, and custom cutters. And there were the people of the horse, buffalo, and teepee. The plains nomads entered the world of Lewis and Clark in the guise of Sioux warriors, Cheyenne traders, and Assiniboine merchants. On the second season of western travel there were the peoples of the Plateau—Shoshone, Flathead, and Nez Perce. Days running the Columbia and weeks at Fort Clatsop showed the explorers a native universe profoundly different from the plains and the plateau. This was the world of salmon, not buffalo; of sea-going canoes, not spirited horses; of plank houses, not teepees or earth lodges. Lewis and Clark did not always understand or appreciate the crazy quilt cultural mix in the West. There was little in their own experience to prepare them for such complexity. But the explorers' journals and other records are filled with the signs of a rich human diversity.

What did Lewis and Clark see? Their journals and maps reveal a West already settled with towns and villages, home to many sorts of people. Add to this a third element. Jefferson's captains found what modern policy planners call large-scale economic development. We might imagine the West's economic map largely empty in 1804. We might emphasize resources not yet exploited. But if Lewis and Clark had that vision of western economies, they soon lost it. From the Missouri to the Columbia the West was crisscrossed with trading trails and exchange routes. Two vast economic systems—the Middle Missouri System and the Pacific Plateau System—spanned the whole West. Through these networks passed every conceivable item: corn from Arikara fields, squash from Mandan gardens, trade guns carried by Sioux middlemen, fancy clothing made by Cheyenne artisans, dried salmon from Columbia River fishing folk, and beargrass baskets from the Chinook villages of the Pacific coast. Lewis and Clark saw Spanish horse tack in North Dakota, found war hatchets they had made at Fort Mandan in the hands of Idaho Indians, and remarked on Boston overalls and British teapots along the Columbia. These huge trade systems and their annual rendezvous were not abstract economic structures of the sort cherished by modern economists. What Lewis and Clark saw was a West bound together by a great circle of hands. Those hands passed around not only fish and fur but songs, stories, and the gift of friendship.

A quick look at the economies of the modern West suggests some enduring continuities with the past as well as some obvious changes. Perhaps the fundamental economic continuity from 1804 well into the twentieth century was the extractive nature of western economies. Westerners—whether native or non-native—harvested the earth. That harvest has changed over time, moving from corn, buffalo, and fish to wheat, cattle, minerals, and oil. And of course we ought not forget tourism, quickly becoming the region's most productive but unpredictable extractive industry. After all, Lewis and Clark were the West's first tourists, seeing all the great sights and writing home to an eager presidential audience. And the explorers were a tourist attraction. Indians came out in great numbers to gape at the odd strangers and their outlandish ways. More than once Clark noted that plains Indians were "continually in Sight Satisfying their Curiossities as to our apperance."[17]

Lewis and Clark were economic geographers. They gave us the first detailed study of business in the West. And in some ways western business has remained remarkably the same. But Lewis and Clark also serve to remind us of how much has changed. What the explorers saw in Indian country were regional markets just beginning to feel the pressure of outside, non-Indian economic forces. While Lewis and Clark did not initiate the western fur trade, the expedition gave added energy to an enterprise already well underway. What the fur trade brought is what large parts of the West have today—extractive industries in a global market place. The trip from fur to oil, from digging sticks to air-conditioned combines and resort complexes is not nearly so far as we might think. And Lewis and Clark help us understand how we began that fateful journey.

Once again we should return to the original question. What did Lewis and Clark see but not always understand in the West? The explorers saw busy communities filled with diverse peoples all linked together by substantial exchange systems, alliances, and friendships. But the captains also saw conflict and violence. One of the most powerful, enduring myths about the West is that it was once a peaceable kingdom, a kind of native Garden of Eden. The American literary tradition has long imagined the West as a paradise where the brave and the venturesome could repeal the past and find the best in themselves. It was as if the very act of moving west promised salvation, renewal, and the death of the past. Thousands of emigrant families bound for Nebraska, Montana, and Oregon all had faith in that gospel. They are the families who fill Jonathan Raban's memorable *Bad Land*, reminding us some gospels are false and that some western journeys do not have happy endings.

At the same time, Jefferson and his successors in the White House knew that the West was a place of terrible conflict, a dark and bloody ground. Jefferson captured that sense of potential violence when writing to Dr. Joseph Priestley. The president described the whole question of the future of Louisiana as "a speck in our horizon which was to burst in a tornado."[18] Louisiana was the West and the very word "tornado" carried all the implications of unexpected change. What did Lewis and Clark see in this country of paradise and sudden death? For the most part, native people offered Lewis and Clark friendship, good company, and open-handed hospitality. But more to the point, the explorers encountered a West riddled with suspicion, hostility, and open warfare. Of all their pieces, the explorers found those marked "Indian diplomacy" the hardest to fit in their Jeffersonian outline. Read again the accounts of expedition diplomacy with the many tribes. Fear and ill-concealed aggression flow from every page. The native

American West had its own rhythms and patterns of personal and communal violence long before Lewis and Clark pitched camp and claimed to talk with the voice of the Great Father. The Lemhi Shoshone headman Cameahwait filled explorers' ears with tales of bloodshed at the hands of well-armed Blackfeet, Atsinas, and Hidatsas. What Cameahwait wanted more than anything else was more guns to extend the violence back upon his enemies. The Lemhi Shoshones had no illusions about the character of their world. It was a country of sudden raids, unexpected kidnappings, and hunger born of fear. When Lewis and Clark called on plains warriors to give up the cycle of raid and counter-raid, the American diplomats got a pointed lesson in western realities. Warfare was the way young men distinguished themselves, and native nations gained respected leaders. Without the discipline of the raid, nations would collapse. And perhaps equally important, raiding meant taking horses—and horses were essential for courtship.

But Lewis and Clark did more than simply record the tracks of violence. As agents of empire they often unwittingly intensified the conflict, extending its reach by new technologies, and giving it a hard ideological edge. What happened at the Two Medicine Fight with the Piegan Blackfeet is an excellent case in point. On the morning of July 27, 1806, while Lewis, George Drouillard, and Joseph and Reubin Field camped in a grove of cottonwoods along the Two Medicine River in present-day north central Montana, violence exploded as several young Piegans attempted to take expedition horses and weapons. In the fight that followed, two Blackfeet were killed. And in a moment of imperial bravado, Lewis took the sacred amulets from the dead men's shields and then hung a peace medal around the neck of one Indian so that "they might be informed who we were."[19] A peace medal had become the calling card of empire. What is important about the struggle between Lewis's small detachment and several Piegans is not the immediate event itself. We need to understand the consequences of the deaths of Side Hill Calf and his friend. Their deaths at the hands of Lewis and Reuben Fields are sometimes credited with being the cause of later violence between American fur traders and the Blackfeet. Popular writers would want us to believe that the bloody deaths of some mountain men were all about revenge. But the truth is more complex and considerably less tidy. The Lewis and Clark Expedition was implicated in that subsequent trader-Indian violence, but not because of simple revenge.

The origins of the violence can be traced to something Lewis said the night before guns barked and knives flashed. Talking with the Piegans around the campfire, Lewis inadvertently dropped a bombshell by declaring that the Blackfeet traditional enemies—the Nez Perces, Shoshones, and

Kutenais—were now united by an American-inspired peace. Even more shocking to Piegan ears was word that these united tribes would be getting guns and supplies from American traders. Here was a threat to Blackfeet dominion that could not be ignored. All of this seemed to come terribly true in subsequent years. By 1807–8 men working for St. Louis merchants were busy trading with Blackfeet rivals. When a former member of the expedition, John Colter, joined in an 1808 battle with Crow and Flathead warriors against the Blackfeet, the message seemed loud and clear. In the face of a massive assault on their plains empire, Blackfeet warriors and diplomats hardly had time to think about avenging the deaths under those three cottonwoods. But they did remember Lewis's words. The explorer was the prophet of violence to come. And the violence did come, and two veterans of the Lewis and Clark expedition paid a high price. John Potts was killed by Blackfeet warriors at the Three Forks of the Missouri in 1808; George Drouillard met the same fate at the same place in 1810.

Long before members of the Corps of Discovery saw what we have come to call the West and tried to make sense of their "seeing," generations of promoters, speculators, and map makers were busy touting eastern frontiers as the Garden of Eden in the New World. Ralph Lane, an English adventurer on the shores of the Carolinas in the 1580s, wrote this to Richard Hakluyt. The eastern margins of North America had "the goodliest soil under the cope of heaven, so abounding in sweet trees that bring such sundry rich and pleasant gums, grapes of such greatness yet wild, as France, Spain, nor Italy hath no greater, so many kinds of apothecary drugs, such several kinds of flax, and one kind of silk, the same gathered of a grass as common there as grass is here. And now within these few days we have found here a Guinea wheat whose ear yieldeth corn for bread, 400 upon one ear, and the cane maketh very good and perfect sugar."[20] Here was an American Nature, at once useful and exotic, of just the sort Jefferson hoped Lewis and Clark would find in the West. Lane's vision of a colonial paradise was repeated again and again as Anglo-Americans pressed over the Appalachians and into the Ohio Country. Albert Gallatin, Jefferson's able and well-informed Secretary of the Treasury, explicitly extended that dream to the West when he argued that the "great object" of the Lewis and Clark expedition was to learn if the country drained by the Missouri could sustain as large a population "as the corresponding tract on the Ohio."[21] Saying "Ohio" meant more than summoning up the image of a grand, navigable river. Ohio was cultural shorthand for a rich and fertile land, one ripe with promise for the young republic.

The many Wests described in expedition journals might have been a caution for those bent on promoting a rural paradise beyond the Missouri. Some parts of the West would have gladdened the heart of any Ohio farmer. Making his way through the Missouri River valley, Clark filled the expedition record with words and phrases like "roleing open and rich," "large butiful prairie," and "charming bottom."²² But most of what Lewis and Clark saw was a country unsuitable to the planting and plowing of the Old Northwest. But the future tide of prospective settlers, land speculators, and railroad promoters did not read what the Corps of Discovery wrote. Instead, they read Nicholas Biddle's *History of the Expedition under the Command of Captains Lewis and Clark.* Like other editors of the day, Biddle took the Lewis and Clark materials and fashioned them into a "connected narrative." He rounded the corners and softened the edges on a West that was not like the East. Members of the Corps of Discovery saw the western landscape through the lenses of previous experience. Those who read Lewis and Clark accounts published after 1814 had to contend with the added experiences and assumptions of a cultured Philadelphia literary editor.

In our own time, thanks to the efforts of documentary editors like Reuben Gold Thwaites, Donald Jackson, and most notably Gary E. Moulton, we can read the very words the explorers wrote. As we now think about what Lewis and Clark saw in the West, the temptation is to overestimate their eastern biases and underestimate our own. Exploration record keepers, writing about whatever place at whatever time, were inescapably rooted in their own cultural ground. By their language alone they saw what were to them new places in the light of old ones. Looking at mounds of earth in present-day Knox County, Nebraska, William Clark fancied them to be "ancient fortifications."²³ John Ordway, hearing the sounds of the Interior Salish tongue for the first time, was reminded about the tale of Welsh Indians lost in the West. But those speculations and imaginings did not prevent either Clark or Ordway from writing accurate descriptions of terrain features or native ways. In the same way, modern readers of the Lewis and Clark journals can be tempted into thinking that the printed page is a photocopy of the past that can be read with neither prejudice nor bias. We sometimes imagine exploration accounts as transparent documents we can look through to see a plain past. But modern readers come to all historical accounts, and especially the Lewis and Clark journals, filled with assumptions about the journey, its meanings, and the country the travelers traversed. Ralph Lane, Thomas Jefferson, and Albert Gallatin are still alive in American culture, preaching the gospel of a garden in the West. So it is easy for us to imagine that Lewis and Clark saw a timeless place, a place beyond change and decay. And we continue to see that place through the eyes of the nineteenth-century painters like Albert Bierstadt and Thomas Moran.

The Lewis and Clark text became the national context. Western artists and illustrators read the Lewis and Clark combat reports and then chose to either accept the myth of the pristine garden or purvey images of stylized, dramatized, and commercialized violence. A century ago the eager press agents of the Northern Pacific Railway published a glorious series of pamphlets extolling the wonders of the West. Thomas Moran appeared there as did other western artists now less well-known. Thomas Jefferson would have loved to leaf through these wonderland guides. They would have convinced him of what he already believed—that the West was a treasure chest bursting with every fantasy known to the super-heated eastern imagination. The solid men of the Northern Pacific; the Chicago, Burlington, and Quincy; and the Great Northern were not about to fill their pages with llamas, mammoths, and Welsh Indians but the impulse was the same. Edna Ferber once said that in Oklahoma anything could happen and probably has. In Jefferson's West, the press agent's West, the line between fantasy and reality was hard to find and easy to transgress. The Lewis and Clark journals, like reports from other explorers, should have been a stiff dose of reality. There were no llamas, the ground shook with buffalo, not mammoths, and the Welsh Indians proved as elusive as ever. But illusion dies hard and the captains could no more escape their dreams than could Jefferson. The words of the president and his captains gave artists, writers, and film makers the boundaries of what William Cronon has gracefully called the "landscapes of expectation." Explorers discovered lands and then employed words to invent futures. The words defined the images, preceded them, and then explained them.

On a clear, bright day in early June 1805 Captain Meriwether Lewis stood beside the Great Falls of the Missouri, the first of five falls at what is now Great Falls, Montana. It was, he wrote, "the grandest sight I ever beheld." The falls were "truly magnificent and a sublimely grand object." Drawn to the water's thunder and spray, Lewis quickly fell into a reverie of "pleasure and astonishment."[24] For a time he struggled to define the falls in measures and dimensions, feet and yards. Words like "beauty," "majesty," and "grand" bumped uneasily against precise counts of distance and drop. But the vocabularies of science and the sublime failed. The falls overwhelmed the imagination. And in a burst of impatience so typical of Lewis, he confessed that he wished for the drawing pencil of Salvador Rosa, the seventeenth-century Italian landscape painter, or the pen of Scottish Romantic poet James Thompson. Lewis said he drafted a hasty sketch of the falls but it has not survived. What has survived are the words—words that continue to mold and shape the way we see the falls and the river. The day after Lewis saw the Great Falls he went up river to Black Eagle Falls. There he saw something so astounding as to seem contrived. In the middle of the river, on the lip of the falls, was an island. On the island a twisted cottonwood supported an eagle's nest. Here was the domestic in the midst of the wild. Some one hundred and twenty-eight years after Lewis stood transfixed by the eagle, the falls, and the river, western artist and Great Falls resident Olaf Seltzer painted the scene. Seltzer knew the view from Black Eagle Falls from first-hand experience. But Lewis's words were part of the artist's cultural inheritance and he composed the scene as the explorer described it. The painting was shaped not so much by field experience as by the memorable power of Lewis's language. This ought not lessen our appreciation of that painting. What that knowledge should do is heighten our awareness of the complex relationship between dreams and expectations, words and images.

All of this should take us back to the original question. What did Lewis and Clark and their companions see in the West? They saw more than they expected, and less. They saw more that was complex and diverse, less that was simple and uniform. They saw violence, ambiguity, and confusion. But they also saw an immense, breathtaking landscape—one that challenged their imaginations and tested their determination. At the heart of the Lewis and Clark achievement is this—that often under the most difficult circumstances weary, hungry men like Lewis, Clark, Ordway, Frazer, Whitehouse, and Gass could find the energy and the intellect to transform what they saw into words for us to read. Donald Jackson once called Lewis and Clark "the writingest" of all American explorers. And write they did. They wrote tirelessly, endlessly, and compulsively. Reading what they wrote offers us the chance to see, if ever so dimly, something of a western landscape now plowed up and paved over. Words had become landscape, and landscape turned once again to words. Explorers carried with them an eastern vocabulary and made it a western one. We read those words and they become our eyes.

Notes

1. David Hackett Fischer, *Historians' Fallacies: Toward a Logic of Historical Thought* (New York: Harper and Row, 1970), 3.
2. JLCE, 2: 215.
3. Ibid., 9: 155.
4. Ibid., 10: 95.

5. Willa Cather, *My Antonia* (Boston: Houghton, Mifflin, 1918), 7.

6. JLCE, 4: 332.

7. Simon Schama, *Landscape and Memory* (New York: Alfred A. Knopf, 1995), 61.

8. JLCE, 2: 369–70.

9. Thomas Jefferson, *Notes on the State of Virginia*, William Peden, ed. (Chapel Hill: University of North Carolina Press, 1955), 18.

10. Adams to Richard Rush, Washington, D.C., July 22, 1813, W. R. Manning, ed., *Diplomatic Correspondence of the United States: Canadian Relations, 1784–1860*, 4 vols. (Washington, D.C.: Government Printing Office, 1940–45), 2: 58.

11. Thomas Jefferson, *Account of Louisiana* (Philadelphia: John Conrad, 1803), 11.

12. Jefferson to the Indian Delegation, Washington, D.C., January 4, 1806, Jackson, ed., *Letters*, 1: 281.

13. Jefferson to Harrison, Washington, D.C., February 27, 1803, Peterson, ed., *Jefferson: Writings*, 1118.

14. Jefferson to Peale, Poplar Forest, August 20, 1811, Peterson, ed., *Jefferson: Writings*, 1249.

15. Joseph J. Ellis, *American Sphinx: The Character of Thomas Jefferson* (New York: Alfred A. Knopf, 1995), 205.

16. Lewis to Lucy Marks, Fort Mandan, March 31, 1805, Jackson, ed., *Letters*, 1: 223.

17. JLCE, 3: 197.

18. Jefferson to Priestley, Washington, D.C., January 29, 1804, Peterson, ed., *Jefferson: Writings*, 1142.

19. JLCE, 8: 135.

20. Louis B. Wright, *The Dream of Prosperity in Colonial America* (New York: New York University Press, 1965), 32.

21. Gallatin to Jefferson, Washington, D.C., April 13, 1803, Jackson, ed., *Letters*, 1: 33

22. JLCE, 2: 291, 275, 310.

23. Ibid., 3: 40–41.

24. Ibid., 4: 283–84.

FIVE

A Moment in Time
The West—September, 1806

Bernard DeVoto once described 1846 as a "Year of Decision." His chosen year was not an endless calendar of days but a series of moments, each decisive in its own unique way. Some moments in time are emblems, signatures of powerful experience and signs of things to come. September 1806 was one of those telling times, an illuminating moment when the American West was in motion—a motion whose direction and consequences was to shape the political and cultural destiny of half a continent.

On that spacious continental stage what were the actors doing as summer edged toward fall? For native people, Europeans, and African Americans, that month spelled change and perhaps a winter of discontent. By freezing motion, by stopping the action we may catch a glimpse of the West poised on the brink of transforming change. From the Saskatchewan to Santa Fe by way of Sitka, from the Columbia and the Purgatoire to St. Louis via Monticello and Montreal, we can hold time prisoner and take the second look that only history can give.

In September 1806 some things seemed timeless, ageless, somehow beyond the hand of change. At Monticello, Thomas Jefferson's westward looking house, slaves and servants hurried to finish the harvest. The master, for once at home, wrote friends on subjects ranging from cucumber seeds to climatology. But September's correspondence offered more than the polite duties of natural history and routine government affairs. The post bag brought two powerful reminders of the West as a land of intrigue and imperial conflict.

On September 12 the president took time to reply to one of his most persistent and troubling correspondents.[1] Joseph H. Daveiss, United States

Attorney for Kentucky and stalwart member of the Federalist party, had been peppering Jefferson with angry letters since early February. Those letters were more than the complaints of a disgruntled representative of the loyal opposition. Daveiss insisted that there was a "damnable plot" to sever the western states from the Union and link a new western republic to Spain. In his first letters Daveiss presented a long list of conspirators including some of the president's closest friends and political allies. Henry Clay, William Henry Harrison, and Attorney General John Breckinridge were among those Daveiss named as enemies of the young American nation. In later lists those politically sensitive names vanished. But however the list shifted, there was always a common cast of plotters. Daveiss identified two— former vice president Aaron Burr, and the current governor of the Louisiana Territory General James Wilkinson. While Jefferson trusted Wilkinson— surely a misplaced trust—there was something about Burr that made Daveiss's charges seem plausible. Burr had been vice president in Jefferson's first administration (1801–5), had failed to secure that position in the second administration, and was now a fugitive from justice after killing Alexander Hamilton in a duel in July, 1804. Daveiss insisted that Burr and Wilkinson were scheming "to cause a revolt of the Spanish provinces, and a severance of all these western states and territories from the union to coalesce and form in one government."[2] While historians have long debated the nature and goals of the Burr-Wilkinson Conspiracy, Daveiss was right about one thing. There was a plot in the making during 1805–6, the leading figures were Burr and Wilkinson, and it did involve the western territories and Spain. Over the summer of 1806 Jefferson had tired of Daveiss's letters but now in September he decided to acknowledge them, if not their assertions. A month later there would be more proof of those claims and then the president would move swiftly against Burr. But for now there was the nagging fear that all was not well for American interests in the West.

The Louisiana Purchase, just three years old, seemed to promise much for the young American republic. But in September 1806 the promise appeared forever deferred. The Purchase treaty had sparked fierce political controversy. There were endless debates in Congress about the wisdom of expansion and even the constitutionality of the treaty. Those rancorous arguments followed Jefferson to Monticello in September. Newspaper criticism of American diplomacy in general and the treaty in particular finally moved the president to draft a long and closely reasoned defense of his policies. Writing to his private secretary William A. Burwell, Jefferson insisted that American representatives had acted in good faith and well within their instructions as they negotiated the purchase boundaries.[3] Three years earlier he had admitted that "our information as to the country is very incomplete."[4] Now in September that information seemed no more complete and the promise of Louisiana offered more threat than reward.

Monticello was Thomas Jefferson's exploration capital. His field headquarters for western reconnaissance was St. Louis. He once called that city "the center of our western operations."[5] September found St. Louis filled with the usual rounds of business and gossip. A month earlier acting territorial Governor Joseph Browne had bitterly complained that "slander flies with the velocity and buzz of the humming Bird."[6] And there seemed much to buzz about. Patrons at William Christy's city tavern passed the time wondering about their territorial governor, General James Wilkinson, now so hastily departed for New Orleans. What about the persistent rumors linking him to the Spanish? And wasn't it just a year ago that he had several days of meetings with the mysterious Aaron Burr? Tavern goers could not have known that Wilkinson was a Spanish spy named as Agent 13 and that in another month this arch-conspirator would denounce Burr in order to save his own skin. And at last the buzz of tavern talk might have turned to Meriwether Lewis and William Clark, now gone two and a half years.

Montreal had been an exploration capital long before Monticello and St. Louis bid for that title. As a center for the French and later the Anglo-Canadian fur trade, the city was home to merchants, traders, financiers, and speculators of all sorts. Montreal was headquarters for the North West Company and fur trade entrepreneurs like Joseph Frobisher and William McGillivray. Over dinner and at meetings of the Beaver Club, fur merchants discussed prices, markets, and the grand sweep of western geography. Those gatherings were virtually graduate seminars in the geo-politics of imperial expansion. The seminar syllabus was always the same—the many ways to expand North West Company influence across Canada to the Pacific. Some in the company later called those plans their "Columbian Enterprise." One of the most attentive students in September, 1806, was the New York fur merchant John Jacob Astor.[7] Since 1788 Astor had been a regular at the Montreal gatherings. What he heard that September and on other visits provided the foundation for the Pacific Fur Company, Astoria, and the creation of the first permanent American commercial enterprise on the Northwest coast.

Montreal, Monticello, and St. Louis—all had a part to play in the drama unfolding up the Missouri and across the mountains. High up the river, at the earth lodge villages of the Mandan and Hidatsa people, the life cycle of the northern plains was about to turn from harvest to preparation for winter. The harvest of corn, beans, and squash had been bountiful—enough to share with those bearded Americans now on their way back home from the great salt sea. A fruitful gathering from the land promised prosperous trading days as Cheyenne, Sioux, Crow, and Assiniboine merchants brought their goods to exchange for what the earth had yielded up.

Far to the West, along the Continental Divide that separates what is now Montana from Idaho, the Lemhi Shoshones were about to join their Flathead neighbors on the annual fall buffalo hunt east of the Divide. It was on just such a hunting journey that the young girl Sacagawea was captured by Hidatsa raiders and put in the way of an unimagined destiny. Now in the fall of 1806 her brother Cameahwait, the band's headman, must have wondered if he would ever again see those pale strangers who had come with his sister the summer before. As he reminded William Clark, Cameahwait cared little for either the pale ones or his long-absent sister. It was the promise of guns that kept alive the hope for a return of those the Shoshones called "men with ash faces." Clark could never forget that night at the Lemhi camp when firelight and shadow danced across Cameahwait's lank face and the chief talked almost mystically about the power of guns.[8] No wonder his warrior name was Too-et-te-con'l, the Black Gun. But now in the fall of 1806 there were no ash-faced men and no guns. Blackfeet, Atsina, and Hidatsa warriors were the ones with the firesticks and the Lemhi Shoshones were as defenseless as ever.

Beyond the Divide, where the land ends and the ocean begins, the Clatsop people of "Dried Salmon" village were busy about their autumn affairs. "Dried Salmon" village, properly called Lä' t' cap in the lower Chinookan language, was located on a branch of the Skipanon River just seven miles from Lewis and Clark's now-abandoned Fort Clatsop. A visitor to the village that fall would have found three large plank houses, homes for twelve extended families.[9] Once greeted by headmen like Coboway or Cuscalar, a stranger—especially a non-native stranger—could not escape the smell in the air. That fall as every fall the air was heavy with the stink of fish gutted and drying. This was the season of the second salmon run, the time of the dog or chum salmon. While the chums were neither as rich nor as oily as the July salmon, they were eagerly caught and prepared. The fish were destined to be traded later that fall to northern and eastern neighbors.

Villagers at Lä' t' cap might have recalled that in late March they saw a ship carrying the colors of the Russian American Company attempt and eventually fail to cross the Columbia River bar. That ship, the American-built *Juno*, was part of the Rezanov Expedition. The ship and its journey along the coast to Spanish California was a reminder of the substantial Russian presence in the north Pacific. At New Archangel (today's Sitka)

Russian American Company general manager Alexander Baranov struggled against an endless round of troubles. Isolation, the threat of starvation, and the constant hazard of native attack made Baranov's world far more uncertain than any Canadian, American, or Spanish rival. What was certain were the demands of hungry mouths and a distant trading company hungry for profit.

These were the things that seemed the same. Gossip, trading, hunting and fishing, visiting, and preparing for winter—the common autumnal tasks in all of North America. From Monticello and Montreal to "Dried Salmon" village and New Archangel the September season made its annual demands. But this was not a static world, immune from change or even catastrophe. In the fall of 1806 the agents of change were everywhere in the West. European and American explorers, soldiers, traders, and adventurers—these men in motion were agents of national states and commercial enterprises bent on dominating the West as an imperial domain. The goods of the Industrial Revolution had come to the region a generation or two before. So had the microbe invasion. Now the nation-state and capitalist enterprise, with bureaucrats, treaties, ledger books, and surveys, was about to line the land and mark its people.

No party of travelers better represented that imperial and commercial thrust than Thomas Jefferson's Corps of Northwestern Discovery, otherwise known as the Lewis and Clark Expedition. The expedition was a Roman legion, an imperial guard sent to scout the fringes of an expanding American imperium. September 1806 found the explorers on the home stretch. They were running with the swift Missouri River current, sometimes making more than seventy miles a day.[10] But this was not quite the triumphant return all on board longed for. Mosquitoes and flies bit faces, hands, and necks. The river glare was sometimes blinding and the juice of ripe pawpaws, accidentally rubbed into the eyes, burned like acid. And there was the embarrassing matter of Meriwether Lewis's gunshot wound. In the previous month Lewis had been accidentally shot by one of his men. While some later writers politely put the wound in his thigh, the truth is the bullet entered one buttock and passed out the other.[11] Captain Lewis came down river belly down, ass up! Such was the price of glory!

But this was not the worst of it. That September the explorers had to face an unyielding fact of continental geography. They had failed in their central mission. The president had made that mission clear on more than one occasion. Lewis and Clark were to find what Jefferson termed "the most direct and practicable water communication across the continent."[12] But Jefferson's dream of a northwest passage up the Missouri, across an easy mountain portage, and down the Columbia to the sea was an illusion. Rivers churned to white water and endless mountain ridges brought the dream face-to-face with harsh reality. And now the president's men had to tell him that a cherished hope was not to be.[13] How could they mint the coin of success out of the base metal of failure?

In the geography of American myth, Lewis and Clark loom as great western heroes. The shadow of failure has been replaced by the radiance of bright reputation. But by shining so brightly they have blinded us to those other autumn wayfarers. No one would have resented that shining more than Zebulon Montgomery Pike. Son of a distinguished career Army officer, Lt. Pike yearned for distinction and recognition. What the Roman poet Ovid once called "the spur of fame" dug deep in young Pike and made him more ambitious than prudent, more trusting than cautious.

Like Lewis and Clark, Pike was a soldier of empire on a mission as complex as any in his age. Lewis and Clark were heading home in September 1806; Pike and his troopers were pointing west and southwest. September found Pike and his modest expedition trekking through present-day Kansas. The party had been out some sixty days, having left St. Louis in mid-July. Pike's mission seemed simple enough. He was to escort some Osage prisoners back home, do a bit of talking with the Kansas and Comanche Indians, and then explore the headwaters of the Arkansas and Red rivers. Such were the instructions written for Pike by his commander, General James Wilkinson. But for Wilkinson nothing was ever simple, nor were things ever what they seemed to be. The instructions for Pike were sure to take him directly into Spanish territory, a fact plainly known and recognized by both the young explorer and his commander.[14] But there was perhaps more here than a dangerous and ill-considered foray on to foreign soil. Wilkinson's motives for sending Pike have long been a source of lively debate. The general did have his eye on developing a private trade to Santa Fe. That desire was so strong that Wilkinson was able to warn off the energetic St. Louis trader Manuel Lisa from making his own New Mexico venture. But Wilkinson may have had more in mind for Pike than a commercial survey of Spanish territory. If Spanish cavalry patrols captured Pike, the event could spark an angry and perhaps violent confrontation between Spain and the United States. In the confusion of a border incident, the Burr-Wilkinson scheme to promote separation and a new western republic might be more easily executed. Young Pike was swimming in waters far deeper than he could know.

In September Pike knew little or nothing of such intrigues. His Kansas days were long and boring. By the end of the month his expedition was camped on the north side of the Republican River, just inside present-day Webster county, Nebraska. From a high rise Pike could see the busy Pawnee villages some two miles south. On September 27 he made a dusty march to the Pawnees. Two days later it was council time. Much to his chagrin Pike discovered he was not the first foreign diplomat to come calling. Spanish flags flapped in the breeze and the best Pike could do was to extract a promise that the Pawnees would not fly them when he was present.[15] For Pike and the men he called his "damned rascals," the road ahead led to confusion, bewilderment, and eventual capture by Spanish forces. But at the end of September that fate was unthinkable. What danced in Pike's head were dreams of honor, advancement, and a rising American empire.

The Spanish flags that so troubled Pike were a vivid reminder that in September 1806 another nation had an exploring party in the field. As early as 1783—the very year American independence was finally secured in the Peace of Paris with Great Britain—Spanish official Juan Gassiot announced that "a new and independent power has now arisen on our continent. Its people are active, industrious, and aggressive. It would be culpable negligence on our part not to thwart their schemes for conquest."[16] By the 1790s, as tensions between Spain and the United States increased over the issue of passage down the Mississippi River to New Orleans, Spanish fears of those American "schemes for conquest" grew more intense. In 1796 the baron de Carondelet, governor-general of Louisiana, was convinced that an American invasion was imminent. Carondelet painted a memorable portrait of his American adversaries, describing them as "determined bandits, armed with carbines, who frequently cross the Mississippi in numbers, with the intention of reconnoitering, of hunting, and if they like the country, of establishing themselves in the Provincias Internas, whose Indians they arm both to further their fur trade and to make the Spaniards uneasy."[17] The aristocratic Carondelet caught the human character of this "prodigious emigration" when he reported that "a little bit of corn, gunpowder and balls suffices them; a house formed from the trunks of trees serves as shelter; they raise camp and then go further inland, always fleeing from any discipline and law."[18] Nothing put in sharper focus the differences between the two nations than their respective definitions of what the Louisiana Purchase really put in American hands. While Jefferson admitted that he was uncertain about Louisiana's real boundaries, he had no doubt that they were broad and far-flung. Spanish officials could not have disagreed more. Manuel Godoy, chief adviser to Spain's King Carlos IV, insisted that the purchase lands were no more than present-day Louisiana, eastern Arkansas, and eastern Missouri.[19] The *Provincias Internas*—the great sweep of territory from

Texas and New Mexico to Kansas and Colorado—was still to be Spain's. But Godoy had not counted on the aggressive energies of the Americans. Perhaps he should have paid more attention to Captain José Vidal who branded the Americans as "ambitious, restless, lawless, conniving, changeable, and turbulent."[20]

James Wilkinson, ever mindful of ways to enhance his value as a spy, skillfully played on those fears. Once Jefferson set his government on the course of territorial expansion and western exploration, Agent 13 had even more to report. While Spanish authorities knew about plans for the Lewis and Clark Expedition as early as December 1802, no action was immediately taken to prevent such a threatening journey. Wilkinson soon made sure that his Mexico City employers did not miss the point. His "Reflections on Louisiana," written in March 1804 and circulated among a handful of Spanish officers, prompted a series of armed efforts to locate and detain Lewis and Clark.[21]

Despite three initial failures, Joaquín de Real Alencaster (governor of New Mexico) and Nemesio Salcedo (military commandant of the *Provincias Internas*) were determined to thwart Lewis and Clark or any other American interlopers. As Salcedo said, "even though I realize it is not an easy undertaking, chance might proportion things in such a way that it might be successful."[22] In mid-June 1806 Real Alencaster organized a massive military force under the able leadership of Lt. Facundo Melgares. The Melgares Expedition counted in its ranks 105 regular troops, 400 New Mexican militiamen, and 100 Indian allies. With a pack train of more than two thousand animals, the expedition was the largest Spanish military party ever to reconnoiter the Great Plains. Melgares's instructions and travel journal have vanished, making a detailed discussion of his enterprise difficult. What has survived are a few scattered documents and several references in the Pike letters and reports.

Sometime in late August or early September Melgares's cavalcade reached the Pawnees on the Republican River. Less than a month later Pike would call on the same Indians. Melgares came looking for Pawnee warriors willing to act as mercenaries against Lewis and Clark. Perhaps what the Spanish officer had in mind was an ambush on the Missouri River. That strategy found no takers and Melgares soon wheeled his expedition toward the Arkansas, the Purgatoire, and home to Santa Fe.[23] Too early to snare Pike, he was too late to capture Lewis and Clark.

Reflecting on the contested border between Spanish territories and the United States, Manuel Godoy dejectedly wrote "you cannot put gates on an open field."[24] Facundo Melgares was a failed gatekeeper. His fellow officer Francisco Viana, adjutant inspector of military forces in the *Provincias Internas*, was far more successful. At the end of July 1806 Viana's substantial armed force was camped on a high bluff along the Red River near present-day New Boston, Texas. His quarry was the Exploring Expedition of the Red River, sometimes known as the Freeman-Custis Expedition. Led by surveyor Thomas Freeman and sometime naturalist and physician Peter Custis, the party was Jefferson's principal probe of the Spanish and American boundary country. Like Lewis and Clark, Freeman and Custis were ordered to pursue many missions. Diplomacy, ethnography, and cartography were just three of the areas to explore in the world between the Red and the Arkansas. Spanish officials were sure to find such a journey both threatening and provocative.[25]

Despite its best efforts, the Freeman-Custis Expedition did not accomplish its full mission. On July 29 Freeman and Custis, along with other members of the party, held a tense meeting with Viana. As Freeman later recalled, Viana explained that his "orders were not to suffer any body of armed troops to march through the territory of the Spanish government; to stop the exploring party by force, and to fire on them if they persisted in ascending the river, before the limits of the territory were defined."[26] The uncertainty of boundaries and the potential for intrigue—here were the defining issues of 1806. Freeman, Custis, and Viana were at a fault line where the earth could shift at any moment. Freeman and Custis took the measure of their own uncertainty and turned back down river. By the last week of August the party was back in Natchitoches, leaving behind a Texas-Louisiana border moving even closer to open conflict.

In the same September that Lewis and Clark were in St. Louis preparing initial reports for Jefferson, Peter Custis was slowly making his way back home to Philadelphia. As the expedition's naturalist, Custis now busied himself making detailed catalogues filled with notations about plants and animals. Those lists amounted to a virtual encyclopedia of the Red River environment.[27] While putting most of his attention toward natural history, Custis may have paused that September to consider what else his journey into the field without gates revealed. It was clearly a world filled with confusion and uncertainty. Political boundaries were vague, diplomatic relations were unstable, and cultural destinies were suddenly insecure. But there did seem to be one frontier certainty, no matter how painful it was to American sensibilities. Zebulon Pike learned the lesson in February 1807 when Spanish troops detained him and marched his expedition south to Chihuahua. Peter Custis had that certainty drilled into him at Spanish Bluff. In any calculation of western futures Spain was not to be counted out. If

Facundo Melgares could lead a grand military reconnaissance through Kansas and into Nebraska three years after the Louisiana Purchase, anything could happen. In the fall of 1806 the lines of empire were by no means set and fixed. Quakes still rumbled along the faults.

The Lewis and Clark, Pike, and Freeman-Custis expeditions represented the official American probes of the West in 1806. But those parties were not the only bands of Americans loose in the big country. Of all those enterprising trappers and adventurers none remains more elusive than Captain John McClellan. On September 17, 1806 Lewis and Clark were on the Missouri at its junction with the Grand River in present-day northwestern Missouri. There they met McClellan leading a party of seventeen traders outfitted with a keelboat and a full supply of trade goods. Once an artillery officer, McClellan had resigned from the Army and drifted to St. Louis. There he became part of Wilkinson's entourage. Since Lewis knew McClellan from previous military service, talk came easily and McClellan soon told a remarkable tale.

As William Clark recorded it in his journal, McClellan was "on reather a speculative expedition to the confines of New Spain, with a view to entroduce a trade with these people." Wilkinson's scheme, so McClellan explained, was for him to build a trading post at the mouth of the Platte River, near present-day Omaha. There McClellan was to hire Pawnee guides for a journey to Santa Fe via the South Platte River. The ex-artilleryman dreamed of entering Santa Fe in grand style. He knew that Spanish officials had long banned trade with foreigners and promptly jailed any who broke the law. To evade the law, McClellan planned to bribe Santa Fe officials while selling trade goods for silver and gold. McClellan expected to open an overland trade with St. Louis—much like what did happen in 1821 after Mexican independence made markets available to American merchants. Lewis and Clark were plainly impressed by McClellan's energy and initiative. Clark confidently predicted success if the scheme was "strictly prosued."[28]

Following McClellan's trail after September quickly takes us from fact to guesswork and slippery speculation. What has survived are a handful of letters and random references in the papers of the Canadian explorer David Thompson.[29] Jefferson's captains probably told their brother officer about the vast beaver colonies in the Rocky Mountains, especially those in the Flathead Valley country of present-day northwestern Montana. It is probable that sometime after parting ways with Lewis and Clark, McClellan made a radical change of plans. He would forgo Spanish silver for brown, furry gold. Following the custom of the country, McClellan's party probably wintered at an old trading post built by St. Louis merchant Regis Loisel at the Great Bend of the Missouri in what is now southern South Dakota. Sometime during the winter McClellan recruited more trappers, including Lewis and Clark veterans Joseph Field and John B. Thompson. By the time McClellan's expedition left its winter camp in March 1807 there were over forty men in its ranks. Using Lewis and Clark information from Field and Thompson, the trappers probably went up the Missouri to present-day Great Falls, Montana and then marched overland via Lewis and Clark Pass to the Flathead country. By July 1807 McClellan evidently had a post on the Flathead River near present-day Dixon, Montana. If this story is accurate, McClellan's men were the first American traders to set up shop in the Rockies.

If they were, they soon discovered they were not alone. Friendly Flathead and Nez Perce Indians told McClellan that a white trader up north was busy selling guns to the Blackfeet. And indeed there was such a man. David Thompson was the North West Company's most wide-ranging explorer. Thompson had worked for some years as a Hudson's Bay Company employee before joining the Nor'westers in 1797. He was now the North West Company's point man in the Canadian drive to dominate the far Northwest. In the summer of 1807 Thompson built Kutenai House on the north end of Lake Windermere in present-day British Columbia. On August 13, 1807 Thompson got a strange and unsettling letter. Dated July 10 and written from a place called Fort Lewis on the Yellow River, the note carried the signatures of Captain Zachary Perch and Lt. James Roseman. Written by someone who assumed that both he and Thompson were on American soil, the letter carried a long list of federal trade and customs regulations plainly aimed at warning off Canadians like Thompson.[30] If Thompson had packed along a roster of American Army officers, he would have been quite confused after paging through it. Perch and Roseman were fictitious names, probably chosen by McClellan, the letter's real author. As it was, Thompson was worried. Writing to North West Company officials that September, he feared that "this establishment of the Americans will give a new Turn to our long delayed settling of this country, in which we have entered it seems too late."[31]

Thompson was not finished hearing from his mysterious and feisty American neighbors. Toward the end of December 1807 there was another note. Written by one Lt. Jeremy Pinch under the date September 29, this letter was both harsh and pointed. It charged Thompson with violating American trade rules and openly selling weapons to hostile Indians. The Canadian was warned that unless he mended his ways, the full weight of the American republic would come down on him. Thompson was not impressed and wrote only a bland reply.[32] With that exchange, John McClellan and his pseudonymous friends Pinch, Perch, and Roseman vanish from the historical record. McClellan may have died at Three Forks in 1810 when Blackfeet warriors killed a number of American traders. But in September 1806 that fate was far off. For John McClellan, ex-soldier and now western adventurer, the West seemed a dream and a promise.

Alexander Henry the Younger, trusted partner in the North West Company, had no such grand dreams. Born in New Jersey in the middle 1760s, Henry was part of a family long connected with the fur business. His uncle, Alexander Henry the Elder, was one of the first English trappers to enter the Winnipeg country and later served as John Jacob Astor's mentor and agent in Montreal. The young Henry entered the fur business early and became a company partner in 1801. As a member of Canada's most aggressive trading company, Henry's life was bounded by ledger book realities—pelts and trade goods, profits and losses. Other Nor'westers had their visions of western empire and acted on them. Henry was a faithful servant content to do the company's bidding.

September 1806 found him doing that bidding at Pembina, his principal trading house.[33] Pembina was located in the far northeastern corner of present-day North Dakota at the confluence of the Pembina and Tongue rivers. The post was headquarters for the Lower Red River Department of the North West Company. Henry oversaw a vast trading system that stretched from the Minnesota woodlands to the westernmost edge of the northern plains. That fall Henry was recovering from a long, demanding journey to the Mandan and Hidatsa villages. His stay at those earth lodge settlements was a reminder that the fur trade on the northern plains had become both part of a global commerce and a point of contention in the struggle for empire. Glass beads from Venice, guns from Philadelphia, knives from Sheffield in England, tobacco from Brazil, vermilion face paint from China, silver jewelry from the German states—all these items found at Indian villages along the Missouri pointed to a world capitalist economy. And the signs of imperial rivalry were just as much in evidence. Henry missed seeing Lewis and Clark but he could not ignore American flags and peace medals. In this war for the hearts, minds, and pocketbooks of the northern plains there were also Union Jacks and coins bearing the marks of the Hudson's Bay Company and the North West Company. It is hard to know if Henry realized what was happening. Did he see the conflicts and ponder their consequences? His richly detailed journal shows only that in the fall of 1806 he fretted about the next trading year. Perhaps it was better to let others plot and plan. But

Henry did have a western appointment as it turned out. And it proved a fatal one. In 1814 he was among a number of Nor'westers occupying Fort George on the Columbia. Fort George had once been Astoria but was now Canadian property. On Sunday, May 22, Henry and several others drowned when their small boat capsized in a sudden squall.[34]

In the fall of 1806 Alexander Henry's life ran in familiar paths. The same could not be said for his more venturesome colleague David Thompson. By that year Thompson was already the most widely traveled of the fur trade explorers. Perhaps no one in the history of western exploration counted more miles on foot, on horseback, and by canoe than Thompson. Along with his Indian wife and children, Thompson spent part of September 1806 at Cumberland House in what is now northeastern Saskatchewan.[35] The days at Cumberland gave Thompson time to mull over instructions given to him earlier that summer. Each July the wintering partners of the North West Company met at Fort William on Lake Superior to plan corporate strategy. Faced with increased Russian and American competition in the Northwest, the company had to move quickly to discover usable routes to the sea. That had been Thompson's task since 1801 and now there was new urgency to his quest. September 1806 found Thompson puzzling over what little was known about the northern Rockies and the upper reaches of the Columbia River. Those puzzles had become the central geographic challenge of his life, and he would not fit the pieces together until 1811. By then it was too late. John Jacob Astor's explorers had already planted his flag and his trading post at the mouth of the Columbia.

For all David Thompson's westward trackings, he was not the North West Company explorer farthest west in the fall of 1806. That distinction belonged to Simon Fraser. Born in Vermont in 1776, young Simon followed his Loyalist family into exile in Canada at the end of the American Revolution. There Fraser became part of the North West Company and was soon caught up in the drive for the Pacific. In the summer of 1805 company partners ordered him west to explore what many thought was the key river of the Northwest. Alexander Mackenzie had called it the Tacoutche Tesse and believed it was the same waterway that American ship captain Robert Gray named after his vessel the *Columbia*. Unbeknownst to any European there were two rivers here, not one. The river Fraser explored—the one that today bears his name—was far more hazardous than the Columbia. Its currents and canyons were a nightmare of rapids and white water. Those hazards nearly cost Fraser his life. Once the Fraser's long and tortured course was known, the Canadians would have an even harder time dealing with American rivals.

In September 1806 Simon Fraser and his party made camp on the south shore of Stuart Lake at the site of present-day Fort St. James in central British Columbia. There they would wait out the winter and then challenge what they thought was the great River of the West. For now Fraser's challenge was to gather adequate supplies for the coming voyage. His autumn letters were filled with complaints about too few men and not enough gear.[36] Had he known the white water hell of the Fraser River canyon he might have asked for even more. What lay ahead for Fraser's party was one of the most dangerous canoe passages in exploration history. As he confided in his journal, "we have to pass where no human being should venture."[37]

September 1806 was a time and space filled with names and ideas in motion. Many of those names remain familiar to anyone with even a passing interest in the history of the West. But the name Nikolai Rezanov has slipped from the memory of even the most assiduous scholars. Count Nikolai Rezanov, grand chamberlain to Tsar Alexander I and a former director of the Russian American Company, was no ordinary imperial bureaucrat. And the accident he suffered in September 1806 while on the way home to St. Petersburg—an accident that hastened his death in March 1807—robbed the Russian enterprise in America of a powerful leader with a compelling and visionary strategy.

By the end of the eighteenth century the Russian commercial and political presence in the north Pacific was substantial. Drawn by the promise of fur, Russian merchants and hunters rushed to the north Pacific. Between 1756 and 1780 Russian adventurers made nearly fifty hunting and trading voyages in Alaskan waters. Intense competition and overhunting eventually drove smaller companies out of business and set the stage for the rise of the monopolistic Russian American Company in 1799. That company and its energetic general manager Alexander Baranov faced a daunting set of problems. From his New Archangel headquarters Baranov looked at a commercial and political empire threatened on every side and in every quarter. Native resistance, inadequate food supplies, uncertain and remote markets, and mounting American and British competition all demanded immediate attention. One problem overshadowed all others. There could be no profit if company employees starved. As Rezanov explained to Baranov in early August 1806, "the shortage of foodstuffs causes diseases, starvation and death among the people." The answer to the supply and market problems was "to extend our commercial operations to find new sources of supply."[38]

The drive to extend Russian America Company commercial operations became the immediate reason for the Rezanov Expedition of 1806 down the

Northwest coast to Spanish California. But this journey had more behind it than a search for grain and beef. In July 1803, just a month after Thomas Jefferson drafted exploration instructions for Meriwether Lewis, the Russian government prepared strikingly similar directions for Rezanov. Both the Russians and the Americans were influenced by Enlightenment ideas about exploration, ideas that connected science, commerce, and national expansion. Like Lewis, Rezanov was instructed to "bring back all kinds of rocks, soils, fossils, salts, sulfurs, metals, woods, plants, seeds, with a description of their use by local inhabitants." Careful observation of indigenous cultures played a central role for both Rezanov and Lewis and Clark. "While in America," so the Russian explorer was told, "you will not fail to note the customs of the inhabitants, their physical characteristics, art, religion, customs, rites, laws, and manners. You will collect reliable information concerning their dress, weapons, dwellings, navigation, housekeeping, food, hunting, fishing, military activities, and domestic animals."[39] Like Lewis and Clark, Rezanov found such guidelines a difficult program to follow.

In late February 1806, after purchasing the ship *Juno* from its Boston captain John D'Wolf, the Rezanov Expedition sailed down the Northwest coast. Paralleling the Lewis and Clark Expedition, Rezanov's first objective was to enter the Columbia River and establish a permanent settlement. On March 31 the *Juno* attempted to cross the treacherous Columbia bar. Like so many other vessels, the *Juno* was caught by what Rezanov described as "the tremendous current and the great breakers in the channel."[40] Had the *Juno* successfully navigated the bar and entered the river, Rezanov and his crew surely would have heard about Lewis and Clark, now gone from Ft. Clatsop only eight days before. But the currents of the bar put a stop to such a coincidence. Four days later the exhausted Russians sailed into San Francisco Bay. They were, by Rezanov's own admission, "ashen and half dead."[41]

Rezanov and his companions spent the next two months in Spanish California. While later romantic poets and novelists made much of the growing affection between Rezanov and Concepción Arguello, the fifteen-year-old daughter of Spanish commandant at San Francisco, the Russian objective was more commercial than emotional. Rezanov left California in late May 1806 convinced that trade with the Spanish territories could solve at least some of the company's food supply problems.[42] Fort Ross, established by the company in 1812, finally brought that promise to life. Rezanov's own life began to slip away in September 1806. An accident on the road to St. Petersburg began a debilitating set of illnesses that finally ended his life in March 1807.

And so the days of September slipped away to a winter fate. Rain, snow, and cold marked the time. By the end of the month Lewis and Clark were in St. Louis shaving their beards, visiting friends, and wondering how to break bad news to Jefferson. Young, over-ambitious Zebulon Montgomery Pike and wily ex-soldier John McClellan each nursed dreams of glory. Facundo Melgares's dreams of glory seemed ever more elusive as he made his way back to Santa Fe empty-handed. Francisco Viana and Peter Custis could only ponder the larger and longer meanings of their meeting at Spanish Bluff. James Wilkinson weathered two military boards of inquiry before his death in 1825. Befitting his role as Agent 13, Wilkinson spent the last three years of his life in Mexico, scheming for land grants and political influence. The Canadians—Henry, Thompson, and Fraser—patiently counted pelts, scouted western routes, and eyed the competition. Nikolai Rezanov, Russia's own Meriwether Lewis, headed home only to meet as tragic a fate along the trail as Lewis would on the Natchez Trace in 1809. And the West's first explorers, native people from the northern plains to Pacific margins, watched the new comers and hoped that little would change. After all, to them, the West was not so much a country of uncertain boundaries and imperial intrigues, but a familiar place fixed in the security of predictable seasons. Was not each September just like the last?

Notes

1. Jefferson to Daveiss, Monticello, September 12, 1806, Thomas Jefferson Papers, The Library of Congress, Washington, D.C. Hereafter cited as TJP-DLC.

2. Daveiss to Jefferson, Frankfort, Kentucky, July 14, 1806, TJP-DLC. The other Daveiss letters to Jefferson are dated throughout January to August, 1806 and can be found in TJP-DLC.

3. Jefferson to William A. Burwell, Monticello, September 17, 1806, TJP-DLC.

4. Jefferson to John C. Breckinridge, Monticello, August 12, 1803, TJP-DLC.

5. Jefferson to Joseph Anderson, Washington, D.C., December 28, 1805, TJP-DLC.

6. Browne to James Madison, St. Louis, August 26, 1806, Clarence E. Carter, ed., *The Territorial Papers of the United States. The Territory of Louisiana-Missouri, 1806–1814* (Washington, D.C.: Government Printing Office, 1949), 14: 4.

7. Extracts from the Journal of Samuel Bridges, Montreal, September 15, 17, 24, 1806, quoted in Kenneth W. Porter, *John Jacob Astor: Business Man*, 2 vols. (Cambridge, Mass.: Harvard University Press, 1931), 1: 412–13.

8. JLCE, 5: 91.

9. James P. Ronda, *Lewis and Clark among the Indians* (Lincoln: University of Nebraska Press, 1984), 186, 191.

10. JLCE, 8: 337–67.

11. Ibid., 8: 155.

12. Jefferson to Lewis, Washington, D.C., June 20, 1803, Donald Jackson, ed., *Letters of the Lewis and Clark Expedition, with Related Documents 1783–1854*, 2 vols., Second Edition (Urbana: University of Illinois Press, 1978) 1: 61.

13. Lewis to Jefferson, St. Louis, September 23, 1806, Jackson, ed., *Letters of the Lewis and Clark Expedition*, 1: 321.

14. Wilkinson's instructions to Pike can be pieced together from letters dated July 18 and 19, 1806, and from Pike's letter to Wilkinson, July 22, 1806, all found in Donald Jackson, ed., *The Journals of Zebulon Montgomery Pike*, 2 vols. (Norman: University of Oklahoma Press, 1966), 2: 117–24.

15. Pike's Speech to the Pawnees, September 29, 1806, Jackson, ed., *Journals of Zebulon Montgomery Pike*, 2: 147.

16. Gassiot to Felipe de Neve Arizpe, Sonora, October 9, 1783, quoted in David J. Weber, *The Spanish Frontier in North America* (New Haven: Yale University Press, 1992), 271.

17. Carondelet to Marques de Branceforte, New Orleans, June 7, 1796, A. P. Nasatir, ed., *Before Lewis and Clark: Documents Illustrating the History of the Missouri 1785–1804*, 2 vols. (St. Louis: St. Louis Historical Documents Foundation, 1952), 2: 439.

18. Ibid., 2: 440.

19. Weber, *Spanish Frontier*, 292–93.

20. Vidal to José Joaquín Ugarte, Concordia, Louisiana, October 4, 1803, quoted in Weber, *Spanish Frontier*, 291.

21. Wilkinson, "Reflections on Louisiana," Jackson, ed., *Letters*, 2: 686–87.

22. Salcedo to Fernando de Chacon, Chihuahua, May 3, 1804, quoted in Warren L. Cook, *Flood Tide of Empire: Spain and the Pacific Northwest, 1543–1819* (New Haven: Yale University Press, 1973), 457.

23. Jackson, ed., *Journals of Zebulon Montgomery Pike*, 1: 415–25. See also: Cook, *Flood Tide of Empire*, 477–83; Weber, *Spanish Frontier*, 294. As a final irony, Melgares was the Spanish officer assigned to escort Pike after his capture.

24. Cook, *Flood Tide of Empire*, 443.

25. Jefferson to Thomas Freeman, Monticello, April 14, 1804, TJP-DLC.

26. Dan Flores, ed., *Jefferson and Southwestern Exploration: The Freeman and Custis Accounts of the Red River Expedition of 1806* (Norman: University of Oklahoma Press, 1984), 204.

27. Custis, "Natural History Catalogues," Flores, ed., *Jefferson and Southwestern Exploration*, 211–79.

28. JLCE, 8: 357–58.

29. The most recent and the most persuasive discussion of the Pinch-Perch-Roseman Controversy is Harry M. Majors, "John McClellan in the Montana Rockies 1807," *Northwest Discovery: The Journal of Northwest History and Natural History* 2 (November–December 1981), 555–611. This essay contains transcripts of all the relevant documents.

30. Perch and Roseman to [David Thompson], Fort Lewis, Yellow River, July 10, 1807, Majors, "McClellan in the Montana Rockies," 601. Majors argues that the Yellow River was McClellan's name for the Flathead River and that Ft. Lewis was named for Meriwether Lewis. McClellan did not know Thompson's name and simply addressed him as a British merchant.

31. Thompson to the Northwest Company, Kutenai House, September 23, 1807, Majors, "McClellan in the Montana Rockies," 598.

32. Pinch to [Thompson], Flathead Lake, September 29, 1807; Thompson to Pinch, Kutenai House, December 26, 1807, Majors, "McClellan in the Montana Rockies," 608–10.

33. Elliott Coues, ed., *New Light on the Early History of the Greater Northwest: The Manuscript Journals of Alexander Henry and David Thompson*, 2 vols. (New York: Harper Brothers, 1897), 1: 424.

34. Ibid., 2: 916.

35. Richard Glover, ed., *David Thompson's Narrative, 1784–1812* (Toronto: Champlain Society, 1962), xci; W. Kaye Lamb, ed., *Sixteen Years in the Indian Country: The Journal of Daniel Williams Harmon 1800–1816* (Toronto: Macmillan of Canada, 1957), 101.

36. W. Kaye Lamb, ed., *The Letters and Journals of Simon Fraser, 1806–1808* (Toronto: Macmillan of Canada, 1960), 239–43.

37. Ibid., 96.

38. Rezanov to Baranov, New Archangel, August 1, 1806, Nina N. Bashkina and David F. Trask, eds., *The United States and Russia: The Beginnings of Relations, 1765–1815* (Washington, D.C.: Government Printing Office, 1980), 455. See also James R. Gibson, *Imperial Russia*

in Frontier America (New York: Oxford University Press, 1976), 9–15.

39. Instructions to Nikolai Rezanov, St. Petersburg, July 22, 1803, Bashkina and Trask, eds., *The United States and Russia*, 373–75.

40. Rezanov to Nikolai Petrovich Rumiantsev, New Archangel, June 17, 1806, Basil Dmytryshyn, E. A. P. Crownhart-Vaughan, and Thomas Vaughan, eds. and trans., *To Siberia and Russian America: Three Centuries of Russian Eastward Expansion, 1558–1867*, 3 vols. (Portland: Oregon Historical Society, 1985–1989), 3: 113.

41. Ibid.

42. Ibid., 140.

SIX

Coboway's Tale
A Story of Power and Places along the Columbia

This is a story about power and places, about what happens when power changes places and then how those places are in turn changed. As befits the best stories, this is a tale of trust and trust betrayed, of deception and the rewards of deceit. And just like the way to Chaucer's Canterbury, this story takes us down twisty roads, across contested borders, and into neighborhoods of what John McPhee calls suspect terrain.

The most compelling stories begin not with people but with places. Here is a geography that seems easy to triangulate. We are at the mouth of the Columbia, nearly two centuries ago. To the north looms Cape Disappointment and Baker Bay. On the south, Point Adams hooks like a bent finger seaward. This is a world of sandy shallows and pounding breakers, where weather changes by the moment and every enterprise flies the flag of uncertainty. Set one marker at the Clatsop Indian village on the tip of Point Adams. When William Clark mapped the point and the village in the winter of 1805–6, he counted eight large wood houses. Perhaps as many as a hundred Clatsops lived at the village they called "where there is pounded salmon." Most likely Coboway and his family lived there.

Pause for a moment and ask—what is the name of this place? If the name is "where there is pounded salmon," then the place is all about Clatsop life and labor and power drawn from the river and fish. But if it is Point Adams, then the lines of power and meaning run east to the Federal City on a very different river and to the name of an American politician. Now run a survey line east and a little south, across the sand hills and mud flats, and into the south channel of the Columbia. Here we are in a narrow, watery trench with hazard all around. To our north is the great Upper Sandbank, sometimes bare in places at low water. To our south is Tansey Point. Mark Tansey Point on your chart. We will have reason to remember it—that point where lines of power crossed and the fortunes of some peoples slid downward. Straight ahead is Youngs Bay and the land that begins at Smith Point. We are back on land now, up over rough and densely wooded ground, and then down to what will soon be Fort Astoria. Set a second marker at Astoria and then run another line southwest across Youngs Bay to the Netul River, now Lewis and Clark River. Follow the river along its marshy, muddy banks—slippery both then and now—to the gate at Fort Clatsop. Pound a final survey stake here, at what Lewis and Clark called their "westernmost station." One last line will finish this skewed triangle. Plot it from Fort Clatsop northwest over marshy ground, across the Skipanon River, through the Brailler Swamp to the sand hills of Point Adams and the Clatsop village. Tie the line at the first post. We have marked and bounded a small world, a wedge of life and landscape.[1] Half a century after William Clark saw the mouth of the Columbia, another American explorer described it as "a perfect Indian paradise in its adaptation to canoe travel, and the abundance of scale and shell-fish."[2]

Coboway's tale was acted out inside those lines but the meanings of the story overrun the limits of the triangle. His story happened in a world every bit as broad, every bit as intricate as the worlds of New York, Washington, Montreal, or Canton. By implication and intrusion, those places had become part of Coboway's world. We should expect a tale as surprising and as unsettling as any told in Bristol or Boston.

Just when Coboway first heard about the Lewis and Clark expedition is lost to us. As an influential man in the Point Adams village he would have been alert to the movements of outsiders. Outsiders might bring violence or chances to trade or both. Coboway's people did not live in some ancient and immense privacy at the very edge of North America. Long before Robert Gray crossed the Columbia bar in 1792 Clatsops and their Chinook neighbors across the river were part of a vast economic and social system that reached north up the coast to Nootka and south down past Cape Blanco. Most important, the trading paths ran up the Columbia to The Dalles and beyond into the Plateau. In the two decades before the arrival of Lewis and Clark, commercial life around Point Adams quickened, stimulated by the maritime fur trade. Although most traders steered toward the safety of Baker Bay on the north shore of the river, the Clatsops did count their share in ironware, pots, and tea kettles. Clatsops became intermediaries, brokers buying and selling to neighbors distant from the river marketplace. A Clatsop story from those years explains it best. A trading vessel grounded on the Columbia bar and broke up. Clatsops salvaged iron, copper, and brass from the wreck. When upriver people heard the news, they hurried to trade. As the storyteller explained, "the people [that is, the upriver people] bought this and the Clatsop became rich."[3]

When Coboway first visited Lewis and Clark's Fort Clatsop, he came as an explorer filled with questions. Who were these *pâh-shish'-e-ooks*, the cloth men? If they were traders, why did they come from the east instead of the west? And what about this beached ship now a-building along the Netul River? Two generations after Coboway, a Clatsop woman named Tsin-istum recalled hearing that her people first feared the Americans, thinking them a party of raiders.[4] The village at Point Adams was in an exposed position and concern about sudden attack was ever present. But for Coboway and others, fear quickly gave way to curiosity. And there was much to be curious about.

Coboway began his explorations on a windy, showery day in early December 1805 and he persisted until the very week the Americans left the mouth of the Columbia in late March 1806. What Coboway learned is part of his story. If he had written an exploration report he might have organized it under two broad headings.

First, there were the familiar things. Coboway and his neighbors knew what traders looked like, how they behaved, what they wanted, and what they had to offer. Coboway came to Fort Clatsop to trade and what he found was what he expected. Some of the earliest Clatsop stories about maritime traders described the bearded, hairy Europeans as bears. But continued contact with the "bears" proved they belonged to the human family. Coboway found men, black and white—clearly men, not bears. The woman and child in the ship-lodge along the river made less sense. Few if any trading vessels carried women and children on board. But just a glance told Coboway that they too were plainly human beings, not spirits and not bears. The things at Fort Clatsop, things that so fascinated interior tribes with less European contact, seemed quite ordinary to Coboway. Guns, pots, fishhooks, metal tools, and textile clothing—these were commonplace all along the lower Columbia. Weeks earlier, Lewis and Clark had seen European-style textiles, tea kettles, pots, and pans at many river settlements. As a trader-come-calling, Coboway got some of those things from Lewis and Clark in exchange for wappato roots, berries, salmon, and elk. One day it was fishhooks and Shoshone tobacco; on other days it was a razor, a moccasin awl and some thread. And once it was a pair of satin breeches. Meriwether Lewis recalled that Coboway was "much pleased" with those fancy pants.[5] While Lewis and Clark did not master the Chinook trade jargon, Coboway and his fellow traders knew a rather select English vocabulary. "Musquit, powder, shot, nife, file, damned rascal, [and] sun of a bitch" might not have pleased some delicate ears but they did the job for trading.[6]

These were the familiar things, the expected landscape. But there was much that seemed strange and not a little unsettling. First there was time, or timing. European traders came to the Columbia first in the spring and then paid a second visit in the fall. By November they were gone. These cloth men came in December, the wrong time and from the wrong direction. Native traders from The Dalles and elsewhere often made the westward journey but white merchants and their ships always came from the Pacific side. White traders who built lodges on land also seemed odd to Coboway. Maritime traders did business on board or immediately alongside their ships. Rarely if ever did they venture on land. But these cloth men—who came at the wrong time and from the wrong direction—seemed rooted to the ground.

Far more puzzling to Coboway was the purpose for the presence of these strangers. Clatsops understood journeys of reconnaissance as part of war or business. But a voyage of discovery launched by a distant nation, a voyage that mixed sovereignty and science, was something new for Coboway to consider. Only once before, in 1792, had Clatsops seen such an expedition when Lt. William Broughton sailed the British exploring vessel *Chatham* up the Columbia to the site of present-day Portland. The Clatsops and their neighbors looked at the American explorers and decided they must be traders. But as Coboway and others soon discovered, these cloth men did not seem to understand the rules of the trading game. The commercial system of the lower Columbia involved both the energetic accumulation of goods and the rituals of exchange. Clatsops were spirited traders who paid attention to the spirits all around them. Trading was a ceremony, a dance of offer and counter-offer that could last an hour or the day. It was both serious business and a great game. The experience itself could be as rewarding as any acquisition.

Lewis and Clark certainly understood bargaining. Whether for land or slaves, horses or tobacco, these Virginians knew first-hand about signals, bids, and breaking the price. They had seen the many ways personal relationships directed and secured commercial transactions. But Lewis and Clark also came from an economic system on the way toward far more impersonal arrangements. Contracts, deeds, letters of credit, lawyers as intermediary negotiators—this was the direction of American capitalism. The ritual ballet of trade practiced by Coboway's people first confused and then infuriated Lewis and Clark. The same day that Coboway paid his first visit to Fort Clatsop, Clark wrote: "I can readily discover that they are close deelers, and Stickle for a very little, never close a bargain except they think they have the advantage."[7] Lewis agreed, calling his native neighbors "great higlers in trade."[8] These were not compliments. Lewis and Clark resented the rules and played the game reluctantly. And of course it did not help that these overland trading captains did not know and did not bother to learn the trade jargon. But Coboway made allowances and became Fort Clatsop's most regular merchant.

Of all the unsettling things Coboway learned, none was more troubling than a new definition of space and the power to define space. First at Fort Mandan along the Missouri and now at Fort Clatsop the American explorers claimed space, squared it, walled it, and made it their own. Along the Netul, the Americans built their station, named it for their neighbors, and then constructed walls and rules to partition the neighborhood. Fort Clatsop was barely done when Lewis and Clark set about to draft their own rules—rules that marked boundaries in time and space, rules about who could come and who could stay. These were rules based not on hospitality or trade but the captains' own notions of convenience and security. At the end of December 1805 the captains let traders like Coboway know that the rules and the spaces were changing. William Clark made this note in his journal to announce the new order of things. "At Sun Set we let the nativs know that our Custom will be in the future, to Shut the gates at Sun Set at which time all Indians must go out of the fort and not return into it untill next morning after Sun Rise at which time the gates will be opened." While those Indians trading the day the rule was issued left the fort "with reluctianc," Coboway readily accepted the dawn-to-dusk business day. After all, it was not much different from the way maritime traders conducted their transactions.[9]

But two days later, on January 1, 1806, the rules changed in dramatic ways. Lewis and Clark sensed that in the first days at Fort Clatsop there had been a contest about rules—what rules and who would rule. This contest asked: where does power live and how will it be expressed? Would it be the spoken words from the village of pounded salmon that carried the day, or would the words on paper from the lodge of the cloth men make the day? Native people exercised domain through rituals that Lewis and Clark could see only as "higle" and "stickle." Jefferson's captains were determined to impose their sense of order and authority on what seemed to them foolish whim and unbridled greed. They would define both power and the places of power. Lewis and Clark wanted to reshape the landscape of time. Days and months once measured in seasons and salmon runs were now to be calculated by calendars and journal entries. What the Americans delivered that first day of January was an elaborate machinery designed to control the roads in and out of Fort Clatsop. Drawing on their military experience, the officers established a complex arrangement of guard posts and sentries. The garrison was commanded to treat native people "in a friendly manner." But "troublesom" Indians or those who strayed into expedition living quarters without permission could be ejected by the Sergeant of the Guard, using whatever force necessary.[10] At least in the minds of the American explorers inside Fort Clatsop, there was no question about who had power. Garrison orders made it plain. Power had changed hands and Fort Clatsop was a changed place. At one spot along the Netul, Coboway was now an outsider in his own country. He entered, traded, and occasionally stayed overnight at the sufferance of others. But even as the ground at this one place shifted, Coboway made his own adjustments. He played by the new rules and gained the grudging respect of the rule makers. Coboway's tale might end right here. Like the Mandan chief Black Cat, Coboway might have slipped off to the wings, just another bit player in a tale larger than he knew.

But the fates and furies were not finished with Coboway. Throughout the winter the American explorers often found themselves on short rations. Game was scarce and expedition hunters were hard-pressed to keep the smokehouse full. In early February George Drouillard, the expedition's chief hunter, killed several elk in the country south of the fort. Having no way to transport the carcasses, Drouillard dressed the animals and cached them in the woods. But leaving so scarce a commodity worried Lewis. "We are apprehensive that the Clatsops who know where the meat is will rob us of a part if not the whole of it."[11] For once such worries were justified. The meat was taken, probably by some Clatsops just as hungry as their neighbors at the fort. Lewis and Clark complained to Coboway and the chief did the appropriate thing. In mid-February he sent a man identified as the elk snatcher to the fort along with two dogs. Dog meat had become a delicacy at the post and the dogs were meant to substitute for the missing elk. But Coboway's plan went suddenly and comically awry. The dogs ran off, perhaps sensing their own destiny.[12] Undeterred, Drouillard went to the Point Adams village, found the dogs, and returned them to the Fort Clatsop cooking pots.[13] Rights and wrongs had been balanced. The case should have been closed. But Coboway was about to get a lesson in just how quickly power could move from one community to another.

To be blunt about it, Lewis and Clark did not like their place on the Columbia. The American explorers hated the weather, loathed the food, and distrusted their neighbors. Fort Clatsop was never the home that Fort Mandan seemed to be. What danced in dreams that winter were the "fat plains of the Missouri." Lewis imagined Fort Clatsop as a prison and once wrote despairingly, "one month of the time which binds us to Fort Clatsop and which separates us from our friends has now elapsed."[14] Counting hard time along the Columbia, Lewis and Clark plotted their escape. Canoes were essential to their return route plans and it was the search for canoes that tangled Coboway in the captains' web of deceit.

Lewis and Clark admired Northwest coast canoes and made careful notes on the makes and varieties they saw along the Columbia.[15] For these captains, canoes meant one thing—safe and efficient transportation. Coboway's people invested canoes with a far greater range of meanings. Canoes were the carriers of life. They bore the freight of trade and war. They were part of the brideprice in marriage. In some places women owned trading canoes. Carriers of life, they were also bearers of death. Canoes held the remains of Columbia River peoples. They were a sign of voyages yet to come. So powerful an object as a canoe required purchase talk of equal gravity. To sell a canoe was not the work of a moment or even a day.

Such considerations were mostly lost on Lewis and Clark. Canoes were useful objects, things needed to make the homeward journey. Throughout the late winter and early spring of 1806 Lewis and Clark did their best to buy canoes. A short stock of merchandise, an even shorter set of tempers, and native reluctance to sell made the process a difficult one.[16] In mid-March, with departure time just a matter of days away, George Drouillard was sent to the Point Adams village to buy canoes. Drouillard returned to Fort Clatsop a day later accompanied by several Clatsops. One man had what Lewis called an "indifferent" canoe and would not part with it even after the captain offered his fancy lace uniform coat in trade.[17] When Drouillard took that coat and some tobacco to a Cathlamet village, he did manage at last to purchase one canoe.[18] Now counting down to their last days at Fort Clatsop, Lewis and Clark were both frustrated and desperate. They wanted to escape, no matter what the price. And Coboway was about to pay the price.

Sometime on Monday, March 17, one of the expedition interpreters—probably Drouillard—approached Lewis and Clark with an ingenious scheme. Lewis put the outlines of this bold plan in his journal, explaining "we yet want another canoe, and as the Clatsops will not sell us one at the price which we can afford to give, we will take one from them in lue of the six elk which they stole from us in the winter."[19] Coboway thought the case of the missing elk had been successfully settled. But now desperation and cultural arrogance worked to reopen the case. Expediency meant more than civility. And besides, how could native ownership of a single canoe be allowed to stand in the way of so important an imperial enterprise?

The following day, March 18, a four-man detail slipped out of Fort Clatsop and headed toward Point Adams. Working unnoticed, the robbers took a canoe and headed back to the fort. At their return, they discovered that Coboway was at the post for a visit. The canoe was hurriedly concealed nearby and brought out only after he left.[20]

The next day Coboway returned to Fort Clatsop, perhaps to ask after the missing canoe. The surviving expedition journals contain no account of any exchange on that question. Instead, the written record reveals an act second in boldness only to what happened the day before. Lewis and Clark presented Coboway with a certificate of good conduct. They also handed him another document—a list of expedition members.[21] There was something prophetic in that exchange. The American adventurers took objects—now a canoe, and later land and gave pieces of paper in return. Lewis once characterized Coboway as "more kind and hospitable to us than any other Indian in this neighborhood." Now he was the victim of a shabby plot.[22] But it would be a mistake to think that Coboway nursed a grudge against his sometime friends at the fort. He might have tossed away the papers, seeing them as signs of trust gone astray. But for the next eight years Coboway kept the list of expedition names—kept the paper as a souvenir, a recollection, perhaps as a connection to the bearded strangers who came and went so suddenly.

This is Coboway's tale. Some of its plot, some of the motion came from the cloth men but this is his story, not theirs. In the years after 1806 Coboway and his people continued their trading and fishing ways. As something of an after-thought, Lewis and Clark gave Coboway possession of Fort Clatsop and its modest furnishings. At least some members of Coboway's family moved in along the Netul, spending the fall and winter seasons inside log walls. Early in April 1811 Coboway's world got a new set of tenants. John Jacob Astor's employees, come over the bar on the ship *Beaver*, settled in and began to build Fort Astoria. This new trading post—what one contemporary called "the emporium of the west"—did not lack for diligent record keepers and scribbling journal makers.[23] Gabriel Franchère, Alexander Ross, Duncan McDougall, and Alfred Seton all put Astoria down on paper. But no one mentioned Coboway. Even though the Astorians made their closest commercial connections with the Chinooks across the river at Baker Bay, Coboway and the Clatsops must have paid at least a few calls on these new cloth men. It was not until December 1813, some three months after Astoria was sold to the North West Company, that Coboway appears again in the surviving record. Alexander Henry the Younger, a Nor'wester who came to the Columbia a month before, noted that Coboway appeared at the post to sell some salmon and elk.[24] And in the months that followed "the old Clatsop chief" made an occasional trip to the place now called Fort George. Henry became his trading partner and perhaps something of a friend. In mid-May 1814 Coboway thought he knew Henry well enough to show him something of great value, something cherished over the years. It was the list of members of the American expedition, dated March 19, 1806—the day after the canoe theft.[25]

Three days after showing Henry the prized paper, Coboway was again face-to-face with Astoria's new owners. There had been an argument about goods missing from the post and Coboway was the one to recover and return them. It was the kind of conciliatory role he had played before. Henry gave Coboway some clothing as an expression of gratitude and then demanded the Lewis and Clark list. Not suspecting what would happen next, Coboway handed over the document. Henry gave the old chief a similar paper declaring the power of the North West Company. Then with great flourish Henry threw the American list—the talisman Coboway had so long cherished—into the fire. The paper blazed up, crinkled, and then crumbled to ash.[26] The message in that moment was unmistakable. Assertions of power, whether between individuals or nations, were as changeable as river currents. Coboway's own part in his tale ends here, with this trick and deception, a fire and the claims of a new paper identity.

But an expanded version of Coboway's tale, one that takes account of the Clatsop future, does not end here. Coboway probably did not live to see the spring and summer of 1829. In that season a fleet from the Hudson's Bay Company's Fort Vancouver bombarded and burned his village. The fire and the looting, and the bland paper explanations offered to justify the violence, are part of Coboway's story as surely as earlier moments of theft and burning.

On March 10, 1829, in bad weather and failing light, the Hudson's Bay Company ship *William and Ann* ran aground while attempting to cross the Columbia River bar. Despite Captain John P. Swan's best efforts, the ship was caught in treacherous currents. Beached on Clatsop Spit, the *William and Ann* split open and was lost with all hands. The next morning the flats around the Point Adams Clatsop village were littered with wreckage and spilled cargo. As they had done for so many years, Coboway's people busied themselves salvaging what they could. News of the wreck reached Fort Vancouver later that day. Dr. John McLoughlin, Chief Factor at the post, quickly sent a rescue party to Point Adams. That expedition found wreckage and cargo but no bodies.[27]

Uncertain how to proceed, McLoughlin and other company officers were ready to let the "melloncholy fate of the crew" slip away. Swan and his men would get their due in the next letter to London and that would be the end of it. But throughout the spring and early summer rumors persisted that Swan and his crew had escaped the Columbia only to be murdered by the Clatsops. Writing a month after the wreck, company clerk Francis Ermatinger predicted that if the murder reports proved true, "we shall have more War."[28] The Point Adams Clatsops did have a reputation as aggressive salvagers and relations between Point Adams and Fort Vancouver had never been friendly. But McLoughlin also recognized that the most persistent rumor monger was an Indian who seemed especially eager to stir up trouble. The Chief Factor bided his time, waiting for more reliable information. That information seemed to come on June 21 when an Indian trusted for his accurate accounts told McLoughlin that the crew had drowned. But, added the Indian, the Point Adams village was filled with company property. Up and down the river word had it that the company was powerless to recover its own goods.

McLoughlin and Chief Trader William Connolly were determined to maintain Fort Vancouver's place of power on the river and soon set on a daring scheme. They organized a large-scale expedition, including the company ships *Cadboro* and *Vancouver*. With more than sixty armed men, Connolly and four other company officers set off towards Point Adams. A messenger was sent on ahead demanding that the Clatsops return company cargo and reveal what they knew about the crew of the *William and Ann*.

Late on the afternoon of June 21 the company flotilla reached Point Adams. A Clatsop headman hailed Connolly's raiders, telling them that all goods would be returned. At that moment the winds switched and the *Cadboro* seemed headed toward the breakers. Hurrying to escape, company men took to small boats and headed for shore. Thinking they were about to be attacked, the Clatsops opened fire. Connolly's men returned the shots and when one Clatsop was hit, most of the other Indians fled. Connolly's men then marched to the village where they ransacked and burned the houses. The Clatsop woman Tsin-is-tum had a starkly simple memory of the event. "My father was killed in the bombardment of the Clatsop village by the ship sent by Dr. McLoughlin."[29] Tsin-is-tum's father was not the only casualty. The attack on Point Adams killed a number of the village's most influential leaders, making recovery even more difficult. The power of a distant place had again flexed its muscle at Coboway's place.

Hard on the heels of the burning and killing at Point Adams came an attack far more deadly and with far greater consequences. From the sixteenth century on, European diseases had wrought unimagined devastation on native North America. Smallpox, influenza, measles, and a host of other afflictions not only killed millions of native people but also assaulted traditional patterns of ritual and belief. Lewis and Clark took note of such diseases on the lower Columbia but it was not until 1830 that the world around Point Adams felt the full burden of a large-scale epidemic. Native people called the illness "the cold sickness" while Europeans described it as "the intermittant fever." Whatever its origin and nature, its results were unmistakable. The disease killed thousands along the lower reaches of the river. Hall Jackson Kelley, who visited the mouth of the Columbia in 1834, reported that he could hear everywhere "the sighs and cries of the misery in the perishing remnants of the Clatsop and Chenook tribes."[30]

Encounters with explorers and traders at Fort Clatsop and Fort Astoria, the attack on the Point Adams village, and the cold sickness were all signs of things to come. They pointed toward a future filled with dispossession and death. But the events themselves, no matter how tumultuous, did not mean that Clatsops of Coboway's generation had either lost their power or their place on the Columbia. Clatsops proved resilient enough to survive in an age of troubles. When the American explorer Lt. Charles Wilkes visited the Point Adams village in May, 1841 he saw a scene much like the one that greeted William Clark almost four decades before. There were plank houses whose interiors reminded Wilkes of ships' cabins. Once inside, he found "pieces of salmon and venison hanging up in the smoke of the fire." What most attracted Wilkes's attention were "figures of men" painted on the bedsteads. The village had seemingly recovered from the 1829 attack and the initial impact of the cold sickness. Wilkes found "numbers of Indians lounging about, and others gambling." But there was one highly visible reminder of the assault twelve years earlier. When Clark saw the Point Adams settlement in 1805–6 it was open to attack. Wilkes found a village surrounded by a strong palisade "made of thick planks and joists, about fifteen feet in length, set with one end in the ground."[31]

If the Clatsops thought that log walls could protect them against threats from the outside, they were badly mistaken. The decade from 1841 to 1851 saw all the hints and signs of power gone to other places come true. The first of those signs to come true appeared in the summer of 1840. Throughout the late 1830s Protestant missionaries had busied themselves evangelizing in the Oregon country. Most of the mission activity was centered in present-day eastern Oregon from Walla Walla to The Dalles. But in 1840 the missionary invasion reached the Clatsops. In mid-July Rev. John H. Frost, a Methodist missionary associated with Jason Lee, decided to establish a post on the Clatsop Plains south of Point Adams. While Frost was impressed with the fertility and beauty of the country, he quickly dismissed his native neighbors as "ignorant, superstitious, and barbarous."[32] Frost was soon joined by lay worker and sometime teacher Solomon H. Smith and his wife Celiast. Known to her English-speaking friends as Helen, Celiast was the second of Coboway's three daughters. Like her sisters Kilakota and Yiamust, Celiast left Point Adams early in life, lived in and around Fort Astoria and Fort Vancouver, and married a non-native man. Later in the fall of 1840, the Frost-Smith mission was reinforced by the arrival of Rev. W. W. Kone and his family. The following year, the missionaries moved their post closer to the Columbia River at a place called New Astoria. For reasons that remain unclear, Solomon and Celiast Smith struck out on their own, building a house and store near Point Adams along the Skipanon River.[33]

While the missionary presence was not large, it was important. Frost estimated that there were about 160 Clatsops living in and around Point Adams. Like his contemporaries, Frost was convinced that native people were lost souls ready to be transformed into regenerated believers and exemplary citizens. Missionaries came armed with an evangelizing program that amounted to a direct attack on traditional practices. If Frost could have had his way, the carved ritual figures Wilkes saw would have been destroyed and replaced with Bibles and appropriate devotional literature. Unlike Astoria's traders, missionaries demanded that native people abandon the old patterns of life and thought. Whether in economy, ritual, or social relations, the model was American cultural Christianity. As one Oregon missionary put it, "we must use the plough as well as the Bible, if we would do anything to benefit the Indians. They must be settled before they can be enlightened."[34]

The threat to Clatsop cultural survival posed by the Methodist mission remains difficult to judge. Frost gained few if any converts and left the mission in disgust in 1843. He was replaced by Josiah L. Parrish, someone who spent more time as a farmer and federal Indian agent than as a missionary. The consequences of western-style agriculture, commercial fishing, and the lumber-sawmill industry were far more visible. Market capitalism was no stranger at Point Adams. The fur trade was a global enterprise and Clatsops and their Chinook neighbors across the river were deeply involved in it. But the fur trade did not have land acquisition as an essential feature of its business strategy. By 1842 farmers associated with the Methodist mission were taking up land south of Point Adams. In the following years, as the Oregon migration swelled, the Clatsop Plains drew additional farming, dairy, and livestock operations. One federal official described the lands south of Point Adams as "open level country with very rich soil." The same official reported that by 1851 "nearly or quite every acre [of the Clatsop Plains] is claimed and occupied by white people."[35] The Clatsop country also contained substantial wood lands, promising wealth to those who measured trees in board feet. Lumbering and sawmilling soon appeared, changing even further the economic face of the lower Columbia. Commercial fishing began in 1829–30, with the first cargoes sold in Boston in 1831.[36]

Point Adams Clatsops understood that these economic activities were remaking their world. Age old patterns of fishing, hunting, and gathering now collided with farms, fences, cows, and mills. Clatsops were especially angry about the disturbing presence of steamboats and two noisy sawmills south of the point. As the Clatsops explained, the boats and the mills frightened away the fish. Without fish, the Clatsops would starve and their ritual world might collapse.[37] Although most whites scoffed at such protests, at least one missionary recognized the consequences of such environmental change. Pondering the future of commercial fishing on the Columbia, Henry Spaulding predicted that "the salmon will be arrested in their upward course by some measure which the untiring invention of man will find out and which is not necessary here to conjecture. That day will be the date of universal starvation of nearly all the tribes of this vast country."[38]

Missionaries, farmers, and mill owners might have been unpleasant neighbors but they lacked the political power to push Point Adams Clatsops off their place. That power belonged to the federal government. Federal Indian policy for the lands west of the Cascades had its formal beginnings in 1848 when Oregon territorial governor Joseph Lane adopted an Indian removal plan much like the one employed against native nations in the Southeast. Lane and his successor John P. Gaines were determined to remove all native people west of the Cascades. In 1850 Oregon territorial delegate Samuel Thurston persuaded Congress to authorize removal treaty negotiations. Anson Dart was appointed Oregon's Superintendent of Indian Affairs and directed to begin the removal process. Once in the territory, Dart quickly realized that removal would be devastating for the Clatsops, Chinooks, and other fishing peoples. As he explained to the federal Commissioner of Indian Affairs, removal was bound to "insure their annihilation in a short time either from want or by the hands of their more warlike neighbors." Dart believed that "small reservations of a few sections and a portion of their fishing grounds" would guarantee Clatsop survival while achieving the goals Washington sought.[39]

When Dart and his negotiating party met with the Clatsops and other coastal Indians at Tansey Point in the first week of August, 1851, he encountered native people who clearly understood their precarious position. Whites had taken up land throughout the Clatsops Plains making hunting and gathering difficult. Commercial fishing, lumbering, and steamboat traffic all disturbed the old ways. But the most serious problem was a rapidly declining population. One federal official estimated that the number of Clatsops had dwindled to about 80 people.[40] An observer at Astoria reported that the Indian villages at the mouth of the Columbia were "mere remnants" of their former size. "It is melancholy indeed," wrote Theodore Talbot, "to witness the tremendous devastation which has here so rapidly followed in the footsteps of the strangers."[41] Having lost so much, the surviving Clatsops were not about to abandon Point Adams. When Dart proposed removal to a small, nearby reservation, Clatsops "interposed many objections to parting with their country upon any terms." What Dart described later as "long and loud complaints" were in fact a carefully reasoned analysis of the Clatsop predicament. Coboway's successors were especially angry about the consequences of the Donation Land Law of 1850. That legislation offered American citizens, or those who intended to become citizens, 320 acres without reference to Indian claims. Even before the land law, white settlers found Clatsop lands attractive. Clatsops argued that the government had "taken possession of their lands without paying them, had allowed white people—many years since—to occupy and buy and sell their country." Clatsops had watched as lands taken under the Donation Law were resold for substantial profit. Despite these complaints, Dart dismissed the Clatsop case as "very unreasonable."

Frustrated by Dart's unwillingness to discuss land issues, the Clatsops switched tactics and threatened to stop the treaty proceedings unless the Indian agent addressed the impact of steamboats and saw mills. Clatsops, known as "close deelers," had once used such delaying tactics to play out the game of trade. Now what Lewis and Clark derisively called "higle and stickle" was part of a larger and more consequential contest. Native negotiators repeated their fears about steamboats and the flight of the fish. When Dart told them he was powerless to halt maritime traffic and dismantle the mills, Indian representatives again changed the agenda. They now asked for two reservations, each about ten miles square. Dart bluntly refused and the entire negotiation dissolved in angry disagreement.

For the next two days Clatsops talked with their Chinook neighbors. While records are scanty, it does seem clear that those conversations produced a new bargaining approach. The Clatsops now asked for a single reservation that encompassed both the Point Adams village and the nearby burying ground. While the request was modest and fit what Dart already had in mind, the discussion hit a sudden snag. Within the proposed reservation were lands claimed by several white farmers. Dart was not about to eject them and proposed instead that the Clatsops "place title to all" their lands with the United States. When the Indians vigorously rejected this idea, Dart angrily issued an ultimatum. Clatsops could either accept the reservation treaty or face an uncertain future without any federal protection. With few alternatives, the Clatsops accepted the reservation treaty and parted with what Dart estimated was about five hundred thousand acres south of Point Adams.[42]

The Clatsops left Tansey Point believing they escaped removal to a distant place. While the proposed Point Adams reservation was small, it did preserve a connection to ancestral places. But Coboway's people had not taken the measure of either congressional politics or the military strategies of the imperial United States. Despite Dart's best efforts, the Tansey Point treaties were not ratified by the Senate. While the reasons behind that inaction have never been clear, Dart believed that the potential cost of the treaties was a powerful argument for the failure to ratify them.[43] But what happened to the Clatsop treaty made little difference in the course of events at either Point Adams or in Washington. Virtually every explorer, traveler, and military observer who visited the mouth of the Columbia noted the strategic importance of Point Adams and Cape Disappointment for the defense of the western United States. Those two sites guarded the entrance to the River of the West. After the settlement of the Oregon Question in 1846, the War Department looked again at the Columbia and its vulnerability to attack from the Pacific. During the 1850s Washington worried about the British navy; later the concerns focused on Confederate raiders. Because the Tansey Point treaties were not ratified, the War Department was free to act on lands at both Point Adams and Cape Disappointment. In 1852 an executive order set aside Point Adams and a portion of Cape Disappointment for the purposes of national defense. Point Adams would now be a military reservation, not an Indian one. A decade later, in the midst of the Civil War, the army began construction of Fort Stevens at Point Adams. Coboway's place now took another name. Fort Stevens honored Isaac I. Stevens, first governor of the Washington Territory. Workers under the direction of Captain George H. Elliott rearranged a portion of Point Adams' landscape, digging ditches, building gun emplacements, and putting up houses and storage sheds. When Julia Gilliss and her husband Captain James Gilliss moved to Fort Stevens in

September, 1866 they saw a settlement wholly unlike Coboway's "where there is pounded salmon." Julia Gilliss described the post as "a beautiful little earthwork bristling with guns and neat as a model, the gravel walks as precise and the grass as green as if they knew they were expected to do their best."[44] Where William Clark had found plank houses, canoes, and salmon, the Gillisses saw two-story frame houses, military equipment, canned goods, and factory-made furniture. The dispossession of Coboway's world now seemed complete.

The Clatsops had lost their place at Point Adams but they did not vanish as a people. Some went to live at the Siletz, Alsea, and Grand Ronde reservations. Others refused to leave familiar haunts and lived out quiet lives on remote parts of the Clatsop Plains. And a handful refused to abandon the Point Adams country. One of those who remained near Point Adams was Toston, a headman who may have played an important role in the Tansey Point treaty talks. Captain Elliott found him living at Point Adams in 1865 and reported that he had "an excellent reputation at the mouth of the Columbia."[45] Two years later, Julia Gilliss found herself one of Toston's customers. "We have living near us," she wrote, "an old Indian named Toastern, who with his pretty daughter brings us fish and berries for sale. We were always glad to hear the musical call 'Olallies' [berries] at our door."[46] Like Coboway at Fort Clatsop, Toston made his way as a trader calling at someone else's outpost of empire.

Perhaps it would be best—certainly from the storyteller's perspective—to conclude Coboway's tale a century after he first met Lewis and Clark. Triangulating Coboway's world in 1905 takes the measure of places transformed and power even more securely in the hands of distant strangers. At the beginning of the twentieth century the United States Coast and Geodetic Survey mapped the mouth of the Columbia. This chart (and the British version published in 1905) starts where we began—at Coboway's village on Point Adams.[47] But in the first years of the new century the village was long gone and in its place was Fort Stevens. The imperial United States, with troops and coastal artillery, now occupied not only Coboway's village but the burial ground nearby. The long-range guns were there to repulse an armada that never came. Take note of the heft of power at Fort Stevens, with its firing pits, Vauban earthworks, and storehouses.[48] Head east and a little south away from the guns and along the tracks of the Fort Stevens branch of the Astoria and Columbia River Railway. Strike out into the shallows beyond Tansey Point, across Youngs Bay, over the bluffs and into the City of Astoria, county seat for Oregon's Clatsop County. In 1905 Astoria was a city of ten thousand—a place where the Columbia River was put in cans and trees became lumber.[49] The Astoria of 1905 was almost as ethnically diverse as the Fort Astoria of an earlier time. Where once there had been Yankees and Scots, Hawaiians and French-Canadians, now there were Finns and Chinese, Norwegians and Danes. From the city of Astoria runs a line southwest back across Youngs Bay, down the banks of the Lewis and Clark River (few called it the Netul anymore) to what was once Fort Clatsop. In 1905 that place of power was a simple farm with a two-story frame house and a scattering of outbuildings. The symbols of empire—flags and guns—had moved to Fort Stevens. From what was once Fort Clatsop walk northwest across marshy ground, over the embankment of the Lexington and Seashore Railway and back to Fort Stevens. A century after Coboway, power was expressed in the guns at Fort Stevens, on the railroad tracks, and at Astoria's canneries and mills.

Power is always unstable, unpredictable—like the sudden currents of a river in flood. And like the river, power is always in motion, sweeping from place to place with restless energy. And as power shifts, it transforms places. The terrain, the very shape of the earth changes. Within the triangle made by Point Adams, Astoria, and Fort Clatsop the earth was shoveled, leveled, blasted, squared, made and remade. Cities, farms, forts, railroads, and canneries—these became the visible manifestations of power in the landscape. But the power that reshaped Coboway's world did not stay at the mouth of the Columbia. It moved on to Portland, San Francisco, Seattle, and back to the District of Columbia. And the reshaping continues. Fort Stevens at Point Adams is now a state park. The National Park Service superintendent at Fort Clatsop ponders problems of parking and visitor security. And Astoria—canneries gone, plywood factories gone—Astoria declines in Victorian gentility selling a Bed-and-Breakfast past to travelers bound for the great Elsewhere.

Coboway's people understood, perhaps better than most, the relationship between power and places. They knew that power lives and moves and has its being in places. At the Tansey Point negotiations, Clatsops told Anson Dart that they were "fully sensible of the power of the government." Clatsops acknowledged that they could be "killed and exterminated" by that power. But they insisted that they would not be "driven far from the homes and graves of their fathers."[50] The road from Point Adams to Tansey Point was not far in miles but walking it Coboway and his people journeyed a long ways from homes and graves. Struck from their own place, they had come to feel the weight of power from other places.

Notes

With thanks for inspiration from Robert Coles and William Cronon.

1. This survey is based on William Clark's notes and maps in JLCE, Atlas, maps 82, 84; 6: 475. See also Charles Wilkes, *Narrative of the United States Exploring Expedition*, 5 vols. (Philadelphia: Carey and Lea, 1845), 4: 322–23, and map sheet 1, "Mouth of the Columbia River . . . 1841."

2. Isaac I. Stevens to George Manypenny, September 16, 1854, in Commissioner of Indian Affairs, *Annual Report for 1854* (Washington, D.C.: Government Printing Office, 1855), 239.

3. Franz Boas, *Chinook Texts*, Bureau of American Ethnology, 20 (Washington, D.C., 1894), 277–78.

4. Olin D. Wheeler, *The Trail of Lewis and Clark, 1804–1904*, 2 vols. (New York: G. P. Putnam and Sons, 1904), 2: 205–6.

5. JLCE, 6: 139, 141, 162–63, 232, 384–85.

6. Ibid., 6: 187.

7. Ibid., 6: 123.

8. Ibid., 6: 164–65.

9. Ibid., 6: 146.

10. Ibid., 6: 156–58.

11. Ibid., 6: 275.

12. Ibid., 6: 299.

13. Ibid., 6: 336, 342.

14. Ibid., 6: 273.

15. Ibid., 6: 262–72.

16. Ibid., 6: 169, 272.

17. Ibid., 6: 414, 416.

18. Ibid., 6: 426.

19. Ibid., 6: 426, 428.

20. Ibid., 9: 278; 6: 429–30.

21. Ibid., 6: 432.

22. Ibid., 6: 444.

23. Alexander Ross, *Adventures of the First Settlers on the Oregon or Columbia River, 1810–1813* (London, 1849; reprint, Lincoln: University of Nebraska Press, 1986), 89.

24. Elliott Coues, ed., *New Light on the Early History of the Greater Northwest: The Manuscript Journals of Alexander Henry and David Thompson*, 3 vols. in 2 (New York, 1897; reprint, Minneapolis: Ross and Haines, 1965), 2: 767–68.

25. Coues, ed., *New Light*, 2: 913.

26. Ibid., 2: 915.

27. McLoughlin to Archibald McDonald, Fort Vancouver, 22 March 1829, Burt Brown Barker, ed., *Letters of Dr. John McLoughlin 1829–1832* (Portland: Binford and Mort, 1948), 6; McLoughlin to McDonald, Fort Vancouver, 17 June 1829, Barker, ed., *Letters*, 12.

28. Francis Ermatinger to Edward Ermatinger, Fort Colvile, 13 April 1829, Lois Halliday McDonald, ed., *Fur Trade Letters of Francis Ermatinger* (Glendale, Calif.: Arthur H. Clark Co., 1980), 123.

29. McLoughlin to the Hudson's Bay Company, Fort Vancouver, 5 August 1829, Barker, ed., *Letters*, 19–21; McLoughlin to the Hudson's Bay Company, Fort Vancouver, 13 August 1829, Barker, ed., *Letters*, 40–41; Wheeler, *Trail*, 2: 205.

30. Fred W. Powell, ed., *Hall J. Kelley On Oregon* (Princeton, N.J.: Princeton University Press, 1932), 326; Herbert C. Taylor, Jr. and Lester L. Hoaglin, Jr., "The 'Intermittent Fever' Epidemic of the 1830s on the Lower Columbia River," *Ethnohistory* 9 (spring 1962): 170.

31. Wilkes, *Narrative of the United States Exploring Expedition*, 4: 322–23.

32. Nellie B. Pipes, ed., "The Journal of John H. Frost, 1840–1843," *Oregon Historical Quarterly* 35 (1934): 71.

33. Robert H. Ruby and John A. Brown, *The Chinook Indians: Traders of the Lower Columbia River* (Norman: University of Oklahoma Press, 1976), 203–4.

34. Elkanah Walker, quoted in D. W. Meinig, *The Great Columbia Plain: A Historical Geography, 1805–1910* (Seattle: University of Washington Press, 1968), 125.

35. Anson Dart to Luke Lea, Oregon City, Oregon Territory, November 7, 1851, in C. F. Coan, "The First Stage of Federal Indian Policy in the Pacific Northwest, 1849–1852," *Oregon Historical Quarterly* 22 (1921): 67.

36. Pacific Northwest River Basins Commission, *Columbia's Gateway: A History of the Columbia River Estuary to 1920* (Vancouver, Wash.: Pacific Northwest River Basins Commission, 1980), 27–28, 33.

37. Dart to Lea, Oregon City, Oregon Territory, November 7, 1851, in Coan, "First Stage," 66.

38. Henry Spaulding to David Greene, October 2, 1839, quoted in Meinig, *Great Columbia Plain*, 134.

39. Dart to Lea, Oregon City, Oregon Territory, February 8, 1851, quoted in Francis Paul Prucha, *The Great Father: The United States Government and the American Indians*, 2 vols. (Lincoln: University of Nebraska Press, 1984), 1: 399. For additional background see Coan, "First Stage," 49–57.

40. Robert Shortess, Census of Clatsop Indians, February 5, 1851, in Ruby and Brown, *Chinook Indians*, 222.

41. Theodore Talbot to His Sister, Astoria, August 2, 1850, in Robert V. Hine and Savoie Lottinville, eds., *Soldier in the West: Letters of Theodore Talbot During His Services in California, Mexico, and Oregon, 1845–53* (Norman: University of Oklahoma Press, 1972), 141.

42. Dart to Lea, Oregon City, Oregon Territory, November 7, 1851, in Coan, "First Stage," 66–67.

43. Ruby and Brown, *Chinook Indians*, 230.

44. Julia Gilliss to Her Parents, Fort Stevens, September 30, 1866, in Priscilla Knuth and Charles J. Gilliss, eds., *So Far From Home: An Army Bride on the Western Frontier, 1865–1869* (Portland: Oregon Historical Society, 1993), 99. The construction history of Fort Stevens is traced in Marshall Hanft, "The Cape Forts: Guardians of the Columbia," *Oregon Historical Quarterly* 65 (1964): 325–61.

45. Captain George H. Elliott, Construction Progress Report, April 25, 1865, in Knuth and Gilliss, eds., *So Far From Home*, 210 n.21.

46. Julia Gilliss to Her Mother, Fort Stevens, April 7, 1867, in Knuth and Gilliss, eds., *So Far From Home*, 124–25.

47. U.S. Coast and Geodetic Survey, "Columbia River: Entrance to Upper Astoria, Sheet 1, 1903," Pacific Northwest River Basins Commission, *Columbia's Gateway: A History of the Columbia River Estuary to 1920* (Vancouver, Wash., 1980), map portfolio; Admiralty Office, Royal Navy, "Columbia River: Entrance to Upper Astoria 1905," ibid.

48. U.S. Army, Corps of Engineers, "Point Adams, Oregon 1885," ibid.

49. Alfred A. Cleveland, "Social and Economic History of Astoria," *Oregon Historical Quarterly* 4 (1903): 130–49; Sam McKinney, *Reach of Tide Ring of History A Columbia River Voyage* (Portland: Oregon Historical Society, 1987), 13–14, 43–50.

50. Anson Dart to Luke Lea, November 7, 1851, in Coan, "First Stage," 68.

SEVEN

A Lewis and Clark Homecoming

It is probably safe to say that neither Thomas Jefferson nor members of the Corps of Discovery ever read anything by the English poet John Keats. But if they had stumbled across Keats' "Preface to Endymion," they would have found these arresting lines. "There is not a fiercer hell than the failure in a great object." Pausing over those sharp words, the president and his men might have had the uncomfortable feeling that the poet was speaking directly to them.

That the Lewis and Clark Expedition was a failure seems almost historical heresy to us. Over the years—and especially in our own time—the expedition has become the preeminent symbol of a nation heading west. Scores of books, films, and museum exhibitions recount the Lewis and Clark story as if it is somehow America's story. There is a kind of triumphant American success story in those highway signs that show Lewis and Clark pointing west. The expedition seems to many Americans the very embodiment of the heroic age. Lewis and Clark are celebrated as pioneer naturalists, cartographers, diplomats, and students of Indian cultures. Several books about the expedition go so far as to assert that only one man died on the journey—an odd claim that not-so-politely ignores the humanity and deaths of Side Hill Calf and his fellow Piegan warrior at the Two Medicine River fight. Others elevate Lewis and Clark to celebrity status. And some seem bent on making the Lewis and Clark story into an American epic filled with manly courage and triumphant nationalism. Unlike us, so ready to claim victory in the "conquest" of the West, Jefferson, his captains, and their contemporaries were not so certain about the expedition and what it accomplished. Because they were uncertain, because they might have felt the sting of the poet's indictment, we need to look again at Lewis and Clark and their homecoming.

On September 26, 1806, just four days after returning from the Pacific coast, Lewis and Clark settled into a rented room in St. Louis and "commenced wrighting."[1] Journal entries, scientific observations, ethnographic notes, and detailed maps—a virtual encyclopedia of the West—needed to be examined, catalogued, and arranged for future study and publication. Surveying the literary remains of their journey, the explorers should have felt the glow of satisfaction that comes from a mission accomplished. But now bathed, shaved, and fed, the president's men had to face an unpleasant reality. They had failed to accomplish the central goal set for them by their commander-in-chief. While they did not need to be reminded of that goal, we do. From its inception, the expedition had but one fundamental objective. As the president put it to Lewis in June, 1803: "The object of your mission is to explore the Missouri river and such principal stream of it, as, by its course and communication with the waters of the Pacific ocean, whether the Columbia, Oregan, Colorado, or any other river may offer the most direct and practicable water communication across the continent for the purposes of commerce."[2] No lines in the Lewis and Clark canon are more familiar than these; Jefferson's explorers probably knew them by heart. And they surely knew they would be judged by them. Whatever else his Corps of Discovery might accomplish, whether in science or diplomacy, Jefferson was intent on having them trace that fabled passage to India.

But as Lewis and Clark learned in what is today Idaho, good intentions cannot transform harsh realities. Geography has a logic of its own, not necessarily amenable to presidential dreams and desires. Jefferson's vision proved illusion at Lemhi Pass and in the bitter snows of the Lolo Trail. Lewis and Clark had failed to find what the president insisted was the essential part of western geography. Now the question was, how to tell him? Like every president, Jefferson did not relish bad news. Torn between accurate reporting and the desire to please their patron, the explorers sought to put the best face on failure. Writing to Jefferson just one day after the end of the journey, Lewis assured the president that the expedition "penetrated the Continent of North America to the Pacific Ocean, and sufficiently discovered the most practicable rout which dose exist across the continent by means of the navigable branches of the Missouri and Columbia rivers." But what the explorer gave with one hand he snatched away with the other. Lewis grudgingly admitted that the passage, while perhaps valuable for the beginnings of the fur trade, was hardly a plain path across the continent. There was no "direct water communication" from Atlantic to Pacific. The northern overland route charted by the expedition would never take the place of the sea lanes around the Cape of Good Hope. As Lewis delicately put it, the overland route was useful only for goods "not bulky brittle nor of a very perishable nature."³ This was another way to say that the "bulky" agricultural products of an American garden in the West would have to reach world markets by some other means. There was a larger failure implied here. No matter how fertile the lands of the West, American farmers would not settle there unless they could sell what they grew in markets across the Atlantic and into the Caribbean. And cut off from the renewing powers of the West, the American republic would inevitably decline into urban squalor and vice. Clark knew those stakes and walked the same tightrope. Writing a letter he knew would be quickly reprinted in western newspapers, the explorer pronounced the venture "completely successful." But there was the inevitable hedge. Clark had "no hesitation in declaring that such as nature has permitted it we have discovered the best route across the continent of North America."⁴ But what nature had permitted was not quite what Jefferson had in mind.

The president's own understanding of the expedition proved equally selective. Jefferson's initial reaction—"unspeakable joy"—at the safe return of the party was reflected in his December 1806 annual message to Congress. Members were told that the expedition "had all the success which could have been expected."⁵ And Jefferson's expectations were grand indeed. The measure of that success, so Jefferson told Congress, was that his captains had found an "interesting communication" across the continent. What the president once sought as a "practicable communication" had now become merely "interesting." By the time Lewis got to Washington in January 1807 Jefferson may have begun to realize that his "interesting communication" was still more hope than reality.

When the expedition was in its earliest planning stages, Attorney-General Levi Lincoln warned Jefferson about the high price of failure. Knowing that administration opponents in Congress would pounce on any hint of defeat, Lincoln counseled the president to plan with great care. Lincoln evidently saw an early draft of expedition instructions, a draft that contained little about ethnography and natural history. Taking the measure of Jefferson's Federalist enemies, Lincoln suggested that those subjects get much more attention. As the Attorney-General saw it, the expedition ought to pursue scientific objectives so that if the passage to the Pacific proved illusory there would still be much to claim. As Lincoln put it with characteristic understatement, if the expedition appeared to advance learning and knowledge "it will by many people, on that account, be justified, however calamitous the issue."⁶

The Attorney-General's suggestions were both politically astute and strangely prophetic. By the summer of 1808 Jefferson had faced the failure of his geographic vision. Not willing to allow this failure to dictate defeat, he now sought to reshape the public image as well as the deeper meanings of the journey. Writing to French naturalist Bernard Lacépède, Jefferson asserted that "the addition to our knowledge, in every department, resulting from that tour, of Messrs. Lewis and Clarke, has entirely fulfilled my expectations in setting it on foot."[7] As the hope of a water passage to the Pacific faded, the image of the expedition as a great scientific enterprise grew brighter. Sir Joseph Banks has been the powerful scientific patron for Cook and Vancouver. Might not Jefferson play that same role in expanding an American empire of the mind? And since knowledge and empire marched hand in hand, a redefinition of the expedition did not necessarily mean abandoning its imperial goals. The president's correspondence with naturalist Bernard McMahon and artist and museum entrepreneur Charles Willson Peale pointed to a new understanding of the expedition's mission. Those letters were filled with lists and descriptions of western plants, animals, and Indian artifacts. Peale, always sensitive to his museum-going audience, observed that "every thing that comes from Louisiana must be interesting to the Public."[8] Levi Lincoln was right. Science—the shape of strange animals, exotic Indians, and useful plants— might rescue the whole venture from oblivion. And it might bolster a presidency sagging under the weight of mounting troubles with England, troubles that would later that year bring the nation to the very edge of war.

The emphasis on scientific accomplishment also fit Lewis's personal conception of what he often called "a darling project of mine."[9] However he had once defined this project, it was now clear that the enterprise was all about scientific discovery. Perhaps now that the journey was over and the passage not found, Lewis imagined the "tour" as a grand walkabout through a vast natural history museum. In the spring of 1807 Philadelphia printer John Conrad issued a prospectus for Lewis's proposed three-volume expedition report. Lewis intended that the first volume be a "narrative of the voyage, with a description of some of the most remarkable places in those hitherto unknown wilds of America." Here was the tale of adventure sought by an enthusiastic reading public. But in keeping with the new emphasis on expedition science, Lewis promised two full volumes packed with ethnography, botany, zoology, and "other natural phenomena which were met with in the course of this interesting tour."[10] In many ways Lewis's prospectus was the formal announcement of a new wisdom about the expedition. Any thoughts about the failed passage now seemed lost in the light of glowing promises of memorable scientific advances.

And at least some of the public seemed ready to embrace this view of the expedition. Michel Amoureux, a French exile living in New Madrid, Louisiana Territory, wrote asking Lewis to put his name on the subscription list. New York artist John T. Jones offered his professional services for engraving maps and plates. Luther Robbins and three of his Maine neighbors had their names added to the buyers list. And Baptist preacher William Woods went so far as to send Lewis $31.00 in advance of publication.

But this public outpouring of confidence in the meaning of the journey had not always been the case. When Lewis and Clark first returned from the West, considerable confusion and ambiguity clouded the significance of their venture. St. Louis townsfolk were bent on celebrating the expedition's homecoming. To that end local officials and merchants hosted a grand dinner and ball at William Christy's city tavern. Those festivities included a round of toasts. Such boozy expressions were an indicator of the expedition's public image, a kind of initial evaluation of what Lewis and Clark had accomplished. And if the drinking at Christy's meant anything, these usually well-informed merchants and traders were not quite sure what Lewis and Clark had done. Manuel Lisa, St. Louis's most aggressive fur trade entrepreneur, was already using expedition information to plot Missouri and Yellowstone river enterprises. But most of the party-goers at Christy's were not nearly so quick to see the relationship between exploration and commerce. The toasts that night praised the nation and the Louisiana Territory, memorialized Christopher Columbus and George Washington, and lauded "the fair daughters of Louisiana." Once Lewis and Clark withdrew, as custom required, they were cheered for "their perilous services to the nation."[11]

But what were those "perilous services" and what did they mean to St. Louis merchants always looking for the main chance? The exuberant townspeople of St. Louis were not alone in their uncertainty about the expedition. Was the great trek nothing more than a grand adventure at public expense? Was the "tour" simply an interesting field problem for two army officers and their pick-up command? When a group of Fincastle, Virginia citizens sent their congratulations, the testimonial emphasized heroic daring against nature's most terrible odds. A passing mention of extending geographic knowledge was overwhelmed by a burst of patriotic rhetoric comparing Lewis and Clark to Columbus and all the greats of the Age of Discovery. St. Louis merchants and Fincastle well-wishers could be excused for their initial uncertainty about the voyage. Jefferson and his captains were equally uncertain about what it all meant. Now in 1808, two years after the return, there might be something to celebrate. Lewis and Clark seemed to be all about science and the expansion of the American mind. As Fincastle citizens said of Lewis and Clark, "your fame will be as pure and unsullied, as of that great man to whom Europe is indebted for a knowledge of our continent; the extent and importance of which, it has been reserved for you to disclose to the world."[12]

Disclosing that knowledge to the world was now the central issue. Jefferson and his contemporaries believed that useful knowledge required publication. The success of the belated Lewis and Clark homecoming celebration depended on the timely publication of Lewis's history of the expedition. By mid-1807 Lewis had made preliminary arrangements for printing the work. Plans were also underway for engraving maps and plates. The only thing lacking was a completed manuscript. In England there was a whole corps of Grub Street literary hacks who transformed explorers' fragmentary notes and journals into finished travel books. Alexander Mackenzie employed the services of William Combe, an experienced ghost writer for other explorers including captains John Meares and James Colnett. But St. Louis had no such literary establishment, nor did any other American city. We should never underestimate the size and complexity of the task Lewis had before him. Arranging and presenting the scientific findings was only part of what needed to be done. Other published exploration accounts offered a narrative with plot, settings, characters, and action. Those accounts were not read as novels but readers did expect to be entertained as well as informed. Lewis had the naturalist's keen eye for detail but as his journal entries reveal, he could not tell a compelling story without wrapping it in a blanket of florid language. When John Conrad, Lewis's Philadelphia publisher, prepared to issue the exploration account written by Lt. Zebulon Montgomery Pike, he warned readers that no book "ever went to press under so many disadvantages as the one now presented to the public."[13] Had Conrad ever received a draft from Lewis, he might have been forced to say the same thing. In 1808 impatient Jefferson prodded Lewis for news. "We have no tidings yet of the forwardness of your printer."[14] The president could only hope that at least one volume might soon appear. A full year after administering that polite scolding to Lewis, Jefferson admitted that "every body is impatient" for the great work to be in print.[15]

If the first Lewis and Clark failure was an intellectual-geographic vision that did not square with western realities, the second failure was far more personal, and as eighteenth-century writers would say, more "tragical." By anyone's measure, Meriwether Lewis was a troubled young man. Ambitious, sensitive, and often brash to a fault, Lewis moved through life as an isolated loner. His few friends worried about his drinking and often unpredictable mood swings. Levi Lincoln warned Jefferson that Lewis might impetuously place himself and the entire Corps of Discovery in harm's way. Lewis was, to be polite about it, a difficult man with an exaggerated sense of self-importance. And now, quite unwittingly, Jefferson put him in an extraordinarily difficult public position. As a reward for faithful service, the president appointed Lewis governor of the Louisiana Territory. Lewis was wholly unprepared, either by training or temperament, for the rough and tumble of territorial politics. Lacking tact and the ability to compromise, he offended virtually every local politician including the powerful territorial secretary Frederick Bates. By the summer of 1809 Lewis's world was coming apart. He was embroiled in half a dozen nasty squabbles; he had stopped writing to Jefferson; he had started drinking once again; his official financial accounts were being questioned by unfriendly Washington officials—and he had not written a single line of his expedition history. Set in this context—the context of profound personal depression and despair— Lewis's suicide in 1809 takes on an added measure of tragic finality. His death meant that the journey would always be told in other voices. What Jefferson called "Mr. Lewis's Tour" would now have less Lewis in it than the president or his secretary ever imagined. Certainly no one felt the fierce hell of failure deeper than Lewis, and his homecoming proved the bitterest of all.

Word of Lewis's suicide shocked but did not surprise Jefferson and those few who knew the explorer well. What did stun them was news that Lewis had made no progress on his literary project. What would the expedition's legacy be if all its efforts did not come to rest on the printed page? In late 1809 Lewis's publisher wrote to Jefferson with the sorry news that "Govr. Lewis never furnished us with a line of the M.S. nor indeed could we ever hear anything from him respecting it tho frequent applications to that effect were made to him."[16] Lewis's failure as an author and his untimely death now set off a complex series of events that finally led William Clark to engage the services of Philadelphia lawyer and writer Nicholas Biddle. Biddle finally brought to press in 1814—almost a decade after the expedition's return—essentially what Lewis proposed as his first volume. Here, in an edition of only 1,417 copies, was the story of the expedition as a glorious western adventure. Biddle did not reduce the Corps of Discovery to a lurid tale of adventure, but he did try to tell a good story. His readers found that story but precious little science. What was supposed to justify the expedition and ensure its place in Enlightenment exploration history was now missing. As Jefferson lamented to Alexander von Humboldt, "the botanical and zoological discoveries of Lewis will probably experience greater delay, and become known to the world thro other channels."[17]

Publication delays, omission of the vital scientific data, and disappointing sales all conspired to produce an expedition record with little public appeal. In the years after the War of 1812 Lewis and Clark were not part of the super-heated nationalism that swept the nation. Stripped of its intellectual achievements, the Lewis and Clark Expedition was increasingly viewed by Americans (when they thought about it at all) as a grand adventure. But this was an adventure without meaningful consequences. No wagon trains rolled along the expedition's overland track. The captains were not pathfinders on the Oregon Trail. American diplomats caught up in the Oregon Question ignored Lewis and Clark, turning instead to the voyages and travels of Captain Robert Gray and the Astorians to justify American claims on the Columbia. When Jefferson summed up what he thought were legal grounds for American rights on the Northwest coast, he did not even mention Lewis and Clark. Writing to cartographer John Melish in 1816, Jefferson explained that "if we claim that country at all, it must be on Astor's settlement near the mouth of the Columbia."[18]

Americans had not lost a national fascination with exploring the West. If anything, the years after Lewis and Clark witnessed the emergence of the explorer as American hero. But Lewis and Clark simply could not compete with the much-publicized exploits of John Charles Frémont and other federal explorers. Jefferson's Corps of Discovery had been eclipsed by Frémont and explorer-scientists like John Wesley Powell, Clarence King, and F. V. Hayden. Eliminated from the scientific lists, Lewis and Clark also fared poorly against popular heroes like Kit Carson, Buffalo Bill, and Jesse James. By the last decades of the nineteenth century the expedition had almost vanished from national memory. The centennial histories of 1876, and the countless school textbooks that followed, had little place for Lewis and Clark. Failure at last seemed complete. Lewis and Clark had been an essential part of the creation of the American West. Now that West had left them behind.

How the expedition was reborn in popular culture at the beginning of the twentieth century to represent triumphant American nationalism, and then re-emerged at the middle of the century to become a household word is a story for another time. The question here is all about failure. How do nations and individuals confront what seems painful failure? How did Lewis and Clark and their patron play the cards dealt to them, whether the hand came by chance or providence? Thomas Jefferson faced the failure of the expedition's central mission by creatively re-defining that mission. Compromise, re-evaluation, and re-definition—these were the ways Jefferson faced failure and tried to transcend it. The fates and furies were not nearly so kind to Lewis. Trapped inside his own life, a life that seemed to spell unrelenting disappointment, there appeared only one way to resolve it all. And so Lewis came home at Grinder's Stand on the Natchez Trace. William Clark's response to all of this was very much in character. Clark was always the understated man, the no-nonsense frontier soldier who did his duty as best he could. Clark recognized the journey to the Pacific as an important turning point in his personal and public life. The journey gave him public office and secured his place as a landowner and businessman. What the Clarks sought as they moved from Virginia to Kentucky, William now found in Missouri thanks to a Pacific tour. And he must have enjoyed the attentions of travelers like Washington Irving, George Catlin, and Prince Maximilian, all eager for his blessing and a share of his knowledge. Catlin went so far as to call Clark "this excellent patriarch of the Western country."[19] But in all of this Clark never claimed that his journey was of vast national significance. The alliance between explorers and press agents had to wait for the likes of Stephen H. Long and John Charles Frémont. For Clark the journey into the West was part of his "tour of duty," a tour that had taken him from the Ohio country to the Pacific and back. The West was simply one more place to carry on with that duty. Facing the failure of Jefferson's geographic vision for the Missouri and the Columbia, Clark drafted his great map to suggest that there might be other rivers to take Americans from Atlantic to Pacific waters. More importantly, Clark refused to define the tour in terms of failure and simply did what he always did—he pressed on with the concerns of his life and the life of his family.

In our own time we may be ready for a more thoughtful Lewis and Clark homecoming. After some two hundred years it may be possible to acknowledge the complexities and ambiguities in a story that has so often been told in the language of triumph and conquest. We might begin that retelling by recognizing that Thomas Jefferson was simply wrong when he repeatedly told his explorers their mission was "single." Even the most cursory reading of Jefferson's exploration instructions reveals an enterprise with many goals, many aims, many missions. While Levi Lincoln had political damage control in mind, he did understand that the consequences of the journey would be measured by more than the discovery of a passage through the western garden. And Jefferson himself came to appreciate the voyage as a venture to be judged by something other than a long sought after passage denied by geography.

We might pay attention to the words of a little-known North West Company fur trader and mariner named Peter Corney. His West was the Pacific Ocean and his exploration voyages were by sea to the Northwest coast. In 1821 Corney published his memoirs, recounting maritime adventure in pursuit of pelts and profit. But in a book filled with stories about

ships, traders, and the native peoples of the Northwest coast, Corney found
a moment to say something remarkably perceptive about Lewis and Clark.
"By the journey of Captains Lewis and Clark across the Rocky mountains
to the Pacific Ocean the whole of that western region is now laid open."[20]
What was it that the American travelers had "laid open?" Corney's words
bring to mind notions of discovery as an act of uncovering what had been
hidden from sight. This was the Enlightenment exploration project that
Jefferson embraced, one that Edmund Burke described as making and then
unrolling the "Great Map of Mankind."[21]

Thomas Jefferson envisioned the Lewis and Clark expedition as part of
the "opening" the West. As European explorers "opened" China, India, and
Africa to global capitalism and imperial rule, so the West would be opened
to the benign presence of the new American republic. The citizens of
Fincastle said as much when they hailed Lewis and Clark for finding a path
to the Pacific "not sprinkled . . . with the blood of unoffending savages."[22]
Exploration was envisioned as part of an Enlightenment enterprise to
reveal the world. What was uncovered would become useful information
for the construction of an American West. Jefferson, Banks, and other exploration patrons imagined they and their discoverers were engaged in writing a grand Book of the World, one that held universal knowledge and
shared it to the benefit of all humanity. No vision was more optimistic and
more ill-fated than this. The knowledge gathered by Lewis and Clark and
their successors amounted to an encyclopedia of the West. The chapter
titles for that encyclopedia were drawn from Jefferson's instructions. There
would be chapters on everything from botany to zoology, from ethnography to mineralogy. And the volumes were to be illustrated with maps, drawings, lists of Indian words, and objects collected along the route. Here was
a guidebook to the West as an American dream. Laying open the West
meant opening the pages of the western book to the hopes and passions of
generations of farmers, ranchers, speculators, and town builders.

But that phrase "laid open" can be read another way. There are other images here, images more violent and disturbing. It was as if explorers held
knives, wielding them to cut open the country so that others might invade
and occupy it. This was exploration as incursion and violation. There is
something more in Corney's words as well. This laying open was also the
act of closing. By "opening" the West, Lewis and Clark advanced the process of closing it. As Brian Harley explains, explorers opened countries to
one set of ambitions and promptly closed them to the dreams of native people as well as rival imperial powers. We can see that by looking at maps and
place names. Lewis and Clark, like other Euro-American explorers, believed

that they were filling up blank spaces on their maps. But Native American maps held no such empty spaces. The blank spaces that so fascinated western cartographers were made by driving Indian dreams and geographies out of the landscape and then inserting Euro-American ones in their place and on their places. Lewis and Clark understood geographic naming as part of a beneficial effort to extend a rational, orderly understanding of the physical world. What they did not appreciate was naming as an act of erasure, appropriation, and possession. Rivers that once had native names came to carry the names of American political figures like Jefferson, Madison, and Gallatin or Enlightenment values like Wisdom or Philanthropy. The maps that recorded those new place names were themselves "inscriptions of political power."[23] Such maps and names laid open the West and re-ordered it according to the passions and desires of those who followed behind Lewis and Clark.

Some fifty years ago Bernard DeVoto challenged Americans to understand the Lewis and Clark expedition as something more than one event in the clutter of human history. "Unless it was just some soldiers that Mr. Jefferson sent to find out how he could protect the sea otter trade from British sea power in case of war," said DeVoto, "it was a turning point in world history."[24] Here, he insisted, were the beginnings of an American empire. The journey of the Corps of Discovery marked the start of a transformation in the political and cultural boundaries of North America and eventually the wider world. Beyond any initial thoughts of failure was the emergence of a global power with imperial aspirations. Jefferson's passage was not to be found but Lewis and Clark began what DeVoto called the passage of American history from an Atlantic phase to a Pacific one. In that scheme of things, and in the lives of peoples and nations, nothing would ever be the same again. The Lewis and Clark homecoming was not the end of the journey. Instead, it marked the beginning of a headlong rush to empire that remade (and continues to remake) the landscape we see every day. If we understand the American terrain as contested ground, it is because Lewis and Clark were part of making it so. Coming to terms with Lewis, Clark, and all those touched by their journey compels us to face our own troubled past and our uncertain present. When we describe the Corps of Discovery we are considering our own history and our own moment in time. Lewis and Clark "commenced wrighting" in the fall of 1806 and we have been finishing their sentences and reading their words ever since.

Notes

1. JLCE, 8: 372.
2. Jefferson to Lewis, Washington, D.C., June 20, 1803, Jackson, ed., *Letters*, 1: 61.
3. Lewis to Jefferson, St. Louis, September 23, 1806, Jackson, ed., *Letters*, 1: 320.
4. Clark to Jonathan Clark, St. Louis, September 23, 1806, Jackson, ed., *Letters*, 1: 326.
5. Jefferson, Annual Message to Congress, December 2, 1806, Jackson, ed., *Letters*, 1: 352.
6. Lincoln to Jefferson, Washington, D.C., April 17, 1803, Jackson, ed., *Letters*, 1: 35.
7. Jefferson to Lacepede, Washington, D.C., July 14, 1808, Jackson, ed., *Letters*, 2: 443.
8. Peale to Jefferson, Philadelphia, October 22, 1805, Jackson, ed., *Letters*, 1: 267.
9. JLCE, 4: 10.
10. Conrad Prospectus, April 1, 1807, Jackson, ed., *Letters*, 2: 394–96.
11. Frankfort, Ky., *Western World*, October 11, 1806, quoted in James P. Ronda, ed., *Voyages of Discovery: Essays on the Lewis and Clark Expedition* (Helena: Montana Historical Society Press), 205.
12. Citizens of Fincastle to Lewis and Clark, January 8, 1807, Jackson, ed., *Letters*, 1: 358.
13. Donald Jackson, ed., *The Journals of Zebulon Montgomery Pike with Letters and Related Documents*, 2 vols. (Norman: University of Oklahoma Press, 1966), 1: xxv.
14. Jefferson to Lewis, Washington, D.C., July 17, 1808, Jackson, ed., *Letters*, 2: 445.
15. Jefferson to Lewis, Washington, D.C., August 16, 1809, Jackson, ed., *Letters*, 2: 458.
16. Conrad and Company to Jefferson, Philadelphia, November 13, 1809, Jackson, ed., *Letters*, 2: 469.
17. Jefferson to Humboldt, Monticello, December 6, 1816, Jackson, ed., *Letters*, 2: 596.
18. Jefferson to Melish, Monticello, December 31, 1816, TJP-DLC.
19. George Catlin, *Letters and Notes on the Manners, Customs, and Conditions of the North American Indians*, 2 vols. 1844 (New York: Dover Publications, 1973), 2: 30.

20. Peter Corney, *Voyages in the Northern Pacific, 1813–1818* (1821; reprint: Fairfield, Wash.: Ye Galleon Press, 1965), 91.

21. Edmund Burke to William Robertson, June 9, 1777, George H. Guttridge, ed., *The Correspondence of Edmund Burke*, 4 vols. (Cambridge, England: Cambridge University Press, 1961), 3: 350–51.

22. Citizens of Fincastle to Lewis and Clark, January 8, 1807, Jackson, ed., *Letters*, 1: 358.

23. J. Brian Harley, *Maps and the Columbian Encounter* (Milwaukee: The Golda Meir Library, University of Wisconsin Press, 1990), 2.

24. DeVoto to Garrett Mattingly, December 2, 1948, Wallace Stegner, ed., *The Letters of Bernard DeVoto* (Garden City, N.Y.: Doubleday and Co., 1975), 305.

Index